SpringerBriefs in Law

SpringerBriefs present concise summaries of cutting-edge research and practical applications across a wide spectrum of fields. Featuring compact volumes of 50 to 125 pages, the series covers a range of content from professional to academic. Typical topics might include:

- A timely report of state-of-the art analytical techniques
- A bridge between new research results, as published in journal articles, and a contextual literature review
- A snapshot of a hot or emerging topic
- A presentation of core concepts that students must understand in order to make independent contributions

SpringerBriefs in Law showcase emerging theory, empirical research, and practical application in Law from a global author community. SpringerBriefs are characterized by fast, global electronic dissemination, standard publishing contracts, standardized manuscript preparation and formatting guidelines, and expedited production schedules.

Gustavo Martins Baini

Objective Limits of Res Judicata

A Fundamental Right Established Between Security and Freedom

Springer

Gustavo Martins Baini
Faculty of Law
Universidade de Lisboa
Lisbon, Portugal

ISSN 2192-855X ISSN 2192-8568 (electronic)
SpringerBriefs in Law
ISBN 978-3-032-07484-3 ISBN 978-3-032-07485-0 (eBook)
https://doi.org/10.1007/978-3-032-07485-0

The original submitted manuscript has been translated into English. The translation was done using artificial intelligence. A subsequent revision was performed by the author(s) to further refine the work and to ensure that the translation is appropriate concerning content and scientific correctness. It may, however, read stylistically different from a conventional translation.

This Springer imprint is published by the registered company Springer Nature Switzerland AG
The registered company address is: Gewerbestrasse 11, 6330 Cham, Switzerland

To Marcia, for daring to leave everything behind and join me and the kids in this adventure in Lisbon. The stability and security of our bond have no limits.

Foreword

This work addresses a challenging topic: What point of a civil court decision becomes legally binding to the parties? The answers vary from considering only the decision's operative part to also considering the legal and factual grounds. But let's be clear: the first solution allows for exceptions, while the second seeks to restrict itself to certain grounds of the decision. This is what the author of this study accomplishes by extending the *res judicata* to the judgment of prejudicial questions if, and only if, certain conditions are met. Written within the context of the civil procedural rights of Portugal and Brazil, the valuable point of the work is to seek a balanced solution, also finding reasons in the *res judicata* of Common Law.

His dialogue with *res judicata* is commendable, both for what it offers us to reflect upon and because it is not common for Latin Country jurist to consider and understand Common Law. Therefore, this study is also a bridge builder in order to obtain a comprehensive view of the problem that deals with.

The author's writing is clear, precise, and open, allowing the reader to access his thinking. His reasons are scientifically sound, and his sources are well presented.

These are, after all, qualities of his thought that we already knew from his PhD program at the Faculty of Law of the University of Lisbon.

Many congratulations to the author.

Faculty of Law of the University of Lisbon
Lisbon, Portugal

Rui Pinto

Preface

This book originates in research I carried out during my doctoral studies in Law at the Faculty of Law of the University of Lisbon (2023–2024), under the guidance of Professors Rui Pinto and Nuno Andrade Pissarra. I was immediately struck by the practical difficulties faced by Portuguese jurists with respect to the extension of the objective effects of *res judicata*. As my research unfolded, it became clear that these difficulties were not uniquely Portuguese: They were also encountered in other European systems, including Italy, France, Switzerland, and Germany.

In Brazil, similar difficulties had long persisted, until they were substantially mitigated with the enactment of the new Code of Civil Procedure in 2015. The legislator's evident inspiration from English and American approaches to the limits of *res judicata* contributed decisively to settling a controversy that had divided courts and scholars for decades—maybe centuries.

I then saw an opportunity to contribute to practitioners within continental European systems by bringing them ideas that may have been prematurely dismissed as incompatible with the Civil Law tradition. The Brazilian experience, however, demonstrates that such adaptation is both possible and fruitful. My expectation is to assist European jurists in broadening their horizons, looking across the Channel and even across the Atlantic. I hope to have shown that the essence of *collateral estoppel*, suitably adapted, fits well within Romano-Germanic legal systems. Above all, I wish for many of the perplexities surrounding the objective limits of *res judicata* to be overcome.

Porto Alegre, Rio Grande do Sul, Brazil — Gustavo Martins Baini

Acknowledgements

To God, who in Jesus revealed the true golden formula between security and freedom.

To Marcia, Martina, and Gabriela—because all good things grow from love.

To Gustavo Pereira, Tutti, Cristiano, and Renata Ritta: because *"navegar é preciso"!*

To my brothers and sisters at Igreja da Lapa, through Pastor Tiago and Ana Rute Cavaco, and to the Rodrigues', Miguel and Isabela, for proving that spiritual family transcends geographical boundaries.

Contents

1 Introduction ... 1
References ... 5

2 The Anglo-American Model: *Collateral Estoppel* and the *Res Judicata* Effect on Issues ... 7
2.1 Convergences Between Common Law and Civil Law: Globalisation of Legal Concepts ... 7
2.2 A Very Brief Historical Outline: The Parallel Path to that of res judicata. From Estoppel to Estoppel by Record and to Collateral Estoppel ... 9
2.3 Critique of Mutuality: Subjective Extension of *Res Judicata* on Issues and the *Non-mutual Collateral Estoppel* ... 11
2.3.1 Bernhard v. Bank of America ... 13
2.3.2 Blonder-Tongue v. University of Illinois: The So-Called Defensive Non-Mutual Collateral Estoppel ... 14
2.3.3 Parklane v. Shore: The So-Called Offensive Non-Mutual Collateral Estoppel ... 15
2.4 Restatement (Second) of Judgements: The Requirements of Non-Mutual Collateral Estoppel, Its Influence on the Brazilian CPC of 2015 and the Possibilities in Portugal ... 17
References ... 20

3 The Roman-Germanic Problems: In Search of the Fundamental Legal Conformation of the Right to *Res Judicata* ... 23
3.1 Some Basic and Useful Definitions ... 23
3.1.1 Adjudicated Case, *Res Judicata*, and Preclusion ... 24
3.1.2 Formal *Res Judicata* and Substantive *Res Judicata* ... 25
3.1.3 Authority of the Adjudicated Case and Exception of the Adjudicated Case: The Problem of Identity Between Two Causes ... 27
3.1.4 Point, Preliminary Issue, and Incidental Decision ... 33

3.2 Values, Legal Principles, and Functions of *Res Judicata* 36
3.2.1 Bauman and the Golden Formula: Security and Freedom in a Love–Hate Relationship 37
3.2.2 More Security or More Freedom? 41
3.2.3 The Golden Formula: Security and Freedom Balanced in *Res Judicata* 47
3.3 Fundamental Right to *Res Judicata*: Constitutionally Adequate Protection Between the Prohibition of Excess and the Prohibition of Deficient Protection 48
References 50

4 Second Outline on the Objective Limits of *Res Judicata*: Defining Criterion – What Becomes Immutable and Undisputable? 53
4.1 The Dispute and Its Object 54
4.2 Topology of *Res Judicata* from the Perspective of the Judgement: In the Ruling or in the Reasoning? 56
4.2.1 Pandectism Between Savigny and Chiovenda 58
4.2.2 (Follows: Topology of *Res Judicata* in the Judgement) Repositioning the Controversy: Ontological Indistinction in the Decision-Making Reasoning and in the Decision of Both the Main Issue and the Preliminary One 63
4.2.3 (Follows: Topology of *Res Judicata* in the Judgement) Repositioning the Controversy: Which Grounds Make *Res Judicata*? *Res Judicata* on a Decision that Resolves Preliminary Issues 65
4.3 Topology of *Res Judicata* from the Perspective of the Initial Petition: Claim and Cause of Action 66
4.4 (Again:) The Dispute and Its Object: Main and Preliminary Issues in Defining the Limit of Material *Res Judicata* 70
4.4.1 The Ambivalence of the Incidental Declaratory Action 72
4.4.2 Brief Considerations About the So-called Extraprocedural Preclusive Effect 75
4.4.3 Brief Considerations on the Competence to Decide Preliminary Issues and the Effects of *Res Judicata* 79
References 80

5 Conclusion: *Res Judicata* and the Binding Force of Preliminary Issues 83
References 87

List of Abbreviations

aC	Before Christ
art.	article
arts.	articles
c/c	combined with
cf.	compare
CPC	Brazilian Civil Procedure Code
CRFB	Constitution of the Federative Republic of Brazil of 1988
CRP	Constitution of the Portuguese Republic of 1974
dC	Anno Domini
ed.	edition
INSS	Brazilian National Institute of Social Security
LINDB	Introduction to the Norms in Brazilian Law
n.	number
p.	page
par.	paragraph
pp.	pages
ss.	following
STF	Federal Supreme Court (of Brazil)
U. S.	*United States of America*

Chapter 1
Introduction

When two parties litigate over the same protected legal interest , it is up to the judge to determine, under the law, who shall be entitled to it . Once this decision is made, it must become stable—if the dispute is indeed to be settled. To allow the allocation of that legal interest to be questioned again would simultaneously encourage litigation and undermine the authority of the State: a true assault on social peace.

This premise is so true that the need to stabilise judicial decisions was felt from the earliest known legal system.[1] True precursors of formal res judicata, the Mesopotamians advocated for the stabilisation of judicial decisions, about 3800 years ago, punishing with a heavy fine and banishment from the judicial function any judge who judged again a case already previously decided, sealed, and deposited (rule VI, § 5°, of the Code of Hammurabi).[2]

Therefore, it is a value recognised for time immemorial: judicial decisions must be stabilised. What has been widely discussed, however, is the *extent* of this stabilisation. That is, what, in a judicial decision, should be stabilised? From when, until when, and to what degree should a judicial decision stabilise? Who should be prevented from questioning what has been decided?[3]

For example, imagine that Maria sues João alleging breach of a wall painting contract and demands that João be compelled to perform the painting he committed to. In his defence, João claims that his consent was not entirely free, and therefore argues that the contract is invalid. Assuming that the judge decides that João's

---

[1] The most developed prehistoric civilizations, such as the Egyptian and Mesopotamian, probably had their legal systems even before writing, and their existence may perhaps be indirectly inferred. However, the historiographic consensus about the oldest legal system rests on the certainty of the two-meter monolith marked with Akkadian cuneiform writing that can be found today in the Louvre Museum – the Code of Hammurabi.

[2] Nieva (2006), pp. 25–30.

[3] These three questions are the subject of studies gathered, respectively, under the signs of "objective limits", "temporal limits" and "subjective limits" of res judicata. Cf. Mendes (1968), pp. 56–63.

G. M. Baini, *Objective Limits of Res Judicata*, SpringerBriefs in Law,
https://doi.org/10.1007/978-3-032-07485-0_1

consent was freely given and condemns him to paint, could he subsequently sue Maria seeking relief from painting the wall on the grounds that the contract has become disproportionately burdensome for him due to the excessive increase in the price of paint? Or if, on the contrary, the contract is declared invalid due to the absence of João's free consent, could Maria initiate a new action alleging the same contractual breach, but seeking damages instead of the painting? And if João had committed to painting walls throughout the neighbourhood, could the decision on the validity of his expression of will in the contract with Maria also affect his neighbours? And if, instead of João, it was a painting company entering standardised contracts for the neighbourhood? Or if Maria discovered new evidence that conclusively refuted João's alleged defect of will? And if this evidence was only discovered ten years after the decision that invalidated the contract? If *res judicata*[4] ensures an indisputable necessity, the extent of its effects remains an open question.

There is a paradox underlying these questions. On the one hand, clearly visible, the stabilisation of the judicial decision promotes social peace.[5] On the other hand, which only becomes apparent if we reflect carefully, the stabilisation of social relations hinders potentially useful adaptations and restricts individual freedom, undermining social peace, in a certain and paradoxical sense. Indeed, social peace requires not only stability but also openness and freedom.[6] There must be room to question and reconsider, to develop and evolve, to explore and even for retreat. A peaceful society needs both structure and freedom; it needs conservation, solidity, and stability as much as transformation, fluidity, and transience.[7]

But a society does not find peace with one foot on the brake and the other on the accelerator, simultaneously and thoughtlessly giving vent to both senses of this paradox. Balance must be found. Knowing to what extent things should stay as they are and from when they should be able to be questioned is the challenge for those who delve into the intricate controversies about the extent of the effects of *res judicata*.

---

[4] Later, in Sect. 3.1.1, an attempt will be made to define more precisely what is meant, for the purposes of this study, by "res judicata".

[5] Moschziscker R (1929), *Res judicata*, Yale Law Journal, 1929, p. 300, cited in Marinoni (2018), p. 49.

[6] Cf. on the subject, for example, Popper and Lorenz (1992).

[7] The contrast between democratic and authoritarian regimes shows that social peace is not only about establishing security, but also freedom. In another context, Konrad Hesse uses this ambivalence to develop his theory of the normative force of the Constitution, identifying, in the contrast between the static and rational norm and the fluid and irrational reality, the importance of the plasticity of the constitutional text and its correspondence to the individuelle Beschaffenheit der Gegenwart ("singular nature of the present", in the classic translation by Gilmar Ferreira Mendes of the work "The normative force of the Constitution", or "individual condition of the present", in the translation by Luís Afonso Heck in "Elements of Constitutional Law of the Federal Republic of Germany") in order to properly shape the political life of a community and ultimately provide that the Constitution has effective normative force. For the German author, stability and dynamism are two inseparable elements of constitutional life. Cf. Hesse (1991), pp. 10 and ss.

This study is particularly dedicated to one of these controversies: the possibility of *res judicata* reaching not only the decision about the primary object of the litigation disputed between the parties but also the decisions that the judge makes to resolve the incidental issues underlying the primary object. It therefore proposes the following questions: Does the stabilising effect of the judicial decision, viewed from the standpoint of the complaint, restrict itself to the decision about the relief sought by the plaintiff, or can it also extend to the decisions about the grounds of the claim? Or, from the perspective of the components of the judgement, does *res judicata* restrict itself to the operative part or can it also reach (some of) its grounds?

On this last dichotomy, restriction of *res judicata* to the operative part *vs.* extension to the grounds, a consideration must be made. Although it is enshrined in the doctrine on the objective limits of *res judicata*, this terminology contributes more to confusion than to clarification. A tweak in the words can help eliminate an important ambiguity: if it is true that attributing the effects of *res judicata* to *all* the grounds raises much suspicion, it must be acknowledged that, in many cases, granting at least *some* of the grounds with the authority of *res judicata* contributes to social peace without significant collateral damage.

This study is dedicated to the search for the identification of these specific grounds and the justification for their stabilisation. It is worth asking: Which grounds should be granted by *res judicata*, and why should they be? The hypothesis to be tested throughout the study is that only those grounds that are contested in the process, effectively litigated and about which there is an express decision can be granted. That is, *res judicata* does not extend to the grounds of the judgement. Strictly speaking, it extends to the decisions that resolve preliminary issues.

Therefore, the question raised in this study is whether a preliminary issue decided in one case can produce any binding effect in other future disputes. If so, why, on what occasions, and under what conditions? The question we intend to explore, in rigorous terms, is the following: Does the decision on a preliminary issue produce *res judicata*? And why?

In order to guide the reader through the red thread that permeates the argument of this study, it is appropriate to express, from the outset, that the hypothesis here supported is that *yes, it is possible to extend the effects of res judicata to decisions on preliminary issues, provided they have been disputed in the process, effectively litigated by the parties and expressly decided by the judge.*[8] Indeed, the words chosen to represent this idea are not random: *res judicata* extends to *(i)* *decisions on* *(ii)* *preliminary* *(iii)* *issues*. That is, there must be an express decision, about a dispute raised in the process on which the main issue depends.

To test this hypothesis, the study is divided into three chapters.

---

[8] This conclusion is reached by a path and with requirements entirely distinct from the solution proposed by João de Castro Mendes, who also considers that res judicata reaches the preliminary issues, but dispenses with the express decision and the requirement of the guarantee of due legal process on the issue, requiring, only, with considerable insecurity, that the preliminary issue to the thema decidendum be "fundamental". Cf. Mendes (1968), pp. 200–201.

In the second, it will be demonstrated that the Anglo-American legal system has followed a path parallel to that of Roman *res judicata* to provide social peace through the stabilisation of judicial decisions, using a different logic, different principles, and consequently producing significantly different results—notably, admitting the stabilisation of decisions on preliminary issues.

This chapter is dedicated to expanding the conceptual horizon of the Romanist legal operator, demonstrating that the concepts and effects traditionally enshrined in continental doctrine cannot be seen as untouchable dogmas—there is a respectable civilisation that has been following a different path.

More than that, it will be sought to demonstrate that the path followed by the Anglo-Americans was adapted and partially adopted in Brazil through the 2015 reform of the Brazilian Code of Civil Procedure (CPC/2015), which can serve as inspiration for other legal systems of Roman-Germanic tradition, such as the Portuguese, as a possible path.

In Chap. 3, the fundamental concepts adopted to keep the vocabulary controlled and ensure, at once, the correct understanding of the present proposal and the possibility of critical dialogue with different views will be exposed.

It will also discuss some of the difficulties that continental doctrine has faced in solving the chronic problem identified in everyday forensic practice related to the doubt about the extension of the effects of *res judicata* to the grounds of the judgement. It will be argued that one of the causes of this problem is the legal criterion to determine the identity of claims—the so-called "triple identity" test, excessively restrictive when compared to jurist's intuitive understanding. It has compelled them to develop a doctrine—that of "authority of the decided case"— to solve it, but with limited success. Instead of this criterion, it will be proposed that the identity between two causes claims be made not on the basis of procedural elements, but rather by those of the decided substantive law relationship.

In this same chapter, it will be sought to demonstrate that the dispute over the objective limits of res judicata involves balancing two antagonistic constitutional values: material legal certainty and procedural freedom. A careful balancing of such values will show that the extension of *res judicata* to decisions on preliminary issues is not only possible, from a constitutional point of view, but mandatory, in order to conform what is here called "fundamental right to res judicata".

Finally, the fourth chapter is dedicated to the search for the *locus* in the process where *res judicata* can be found. The binomials enshrined in doctrine will be examined: in relation to the initial pleading, does *res judicata* limit itself to the claim or extend to the cause of action? In relation to the judgement, does *res judicata* restrict itself to the ruling or reach the grounds? Instead of these two, two other binomials will be proposed capable of identifying *res judicata* in the process: in the claim/ruling (main issue) and in the causes of action/grounds (preliminary issue).

In the course of this last chapter, two great nineteenth-century doctrinarians will be called to dialogue as representatives of the precursors of the controversy. Chiovenda, defending the restriction of *res judicata* to the claim, and Savigny, considering it extensive to the grounds. An attempt will be made to identify the roots of this divergence and, in the end, reposition the controversy to propose a possible convergence.

Still in the last chapter, it will be concluded that the object of res judicata is the object of the dispute, that is, the subject matter about which the parties claim jurisdiction and over which they are assured the *due process of law*, whether such object is restricted to the claim/ruling (main issue) or reaches the cause of action/grounds (preliminary issue).

References

Hesse K (1991) A força normativa da Constituição. Sergio Antonio Fabris Editor, Porto Alegre
Marinoni LG (2018) Coisa julgada sobre questão. Revista dos Tribunais, São Paulo
Mendes JC (1968) Limites objectivos do caso julgado em processo civil. Ática, Lisboa
Nieva JF (2006) La cosa juzgada. Atelier, Barcelona
Popper K, Lorenz K (1992) El porvenir está abierto. Tusquets, Barcelona

Chapter 2
The Anglo-American Model: *Collateral Estoppel* and the *Res Judicata* Effect on Issues

2.1 Convergences Between Common Law and Civil Law: Globalisation of Legal Concepts

The two major legal traditions, also referred to as "families", methodologically separated for a better understanding of comparative law scholars,[1] have been gradually converging.[2]

The proliferation of *statutes* in Anglo-American systems and the increasing importance of judicial precedents in Roman-Germanic systems are examples of this.[3] Many other examples can be given: the semantic opening of legislative texts in recent decades and the drafting of a written Constitution for England are just two more.

There is one point, however, where the tradition of *Common Law* significantly touched *Civil Law* in terms of the extent of the effects of *res judicata*.

Brazilian *res judicata* was greatly influenced by the Anglo-American *collateral estoppel* following the enactment of the Brazilian Code of Civil Procedure in 2015. It is impossible not to notice[4] the similarities between §§ 1 and 2 of art. 503 of this

---

[1] David (2002).

[2] One of the first to notice this was Calabresi (1982). In the opposite sense, Bersier et al. (2022).

[3] Not by chance Neil MacCormick and Robert Summers gathered some of the most prominent theorists on the theory of interpretation of their time, from each of the two traditions, in a fundamental work on the subject, organising it in two volumes published, respectively, in 1991 and 1997, significantly called Interpreting precedents and Interpreting statutes.

[4] As, indeed, Luiz Guilherme Marinoni (2016) noticed, specifically in § 7 of this article.

G. M. Baini, *Objective Limits of Res Judicata*, SpringerBriefs in Law,
https://doi.org/10.1007/978-3-032-07485-0_2

Code[5] and § 27 of the *Restatement (Second) of Judgements,*[6] the latter aligned with the most representative precedents of the *U. S. Supreme Court* of the twentieth century on the subject.

The effective practice of *collateral estoppel* in *Common Law* sends a powerful message that it is possible to extend the effects of *res judicata* beyond the ruling, without this causing the insecurity and perplexity that Portuguese judges and lawyers have been striving to overcome.

Through this influence, the Brazilian legal system has resolved with considerable certainty the problem of extending the effects of *res judicata* to the grounds.[7] One of the aims of this study is to provide Portuguese legal practitioners with points of support to, following this line, achieve similar certainty in one of the most challenging topics of judicial practice in terms of procedural theory.[8]

The idea of this chapter is not to suggest the importation of the American model. It is believed that the ideas developed in the next chapter will provide greater comfort to the Portuguese legal practitioner in overcoming the current paradigm than simply replicating, without adaptations, a model that has such substantially different foundations—as should become clear in this chapter. However, it is undeniable that knowing the Anglo-American experience broadens horizons, and thus increases receptivity for such overcoming.

Therefore, in this first chapter, brief lines will be exposed to demonstrate how the Anglo-American system dealt so differently with the problem of the need for stabilisation of judicial decisions, leading them to safer conclusions than the traditionally Roman-Germanic ones.

---

[5] Art. 503. The decision that judges total or partially the merit has the force of law within the limits of the main issue expressly decided. § 1° The provision in the caput applies to the resolution of a preliminary issue, decided expressly and incidentally in the process, if: I - this resolution depends on the judgement of the merit; II - there has been prior and effective contradiction about it, not applying in the case of default; III - the court has competence in reason of the matter and the person to resolve it as a main issue. § 2° The hypothesis of § 1° does not apply if there are restrictions in the process. evidentiary or cognitive limitations that prevent a deeper analysis of the preliminary issue.

[6] When an issue of fact or law is actually litigated and determined by a valid and final judgment, and the determination is essential to the judgment, the determination is conclusive in a subsequent action between the parties, whether on the same or a different claim.

[7] Baini (2024a, b).

[8] This is evident, for example, in the significant, alarming and humorous title of José Lebre de Freitas's essay: "An octopus called authority of the decided case." Freitas (2019).

2.2 A Very Brief Historical Outline: The Parallel Path to that of res judicata. From Estoppel to Estoppel by Record and to Collateral Estoppel

The doctrine of *res judicata* developed in countries of the *civil law* tradition originates from ancient Roman Law, dating back to the *Digest*, also known as *Pandects.* The *Digest*, as is known, is part of the *Corpus Iuris Civilis,* the Justinian Code produced in the sixth century AD. Although it represents a compilation of older sources, the scarcity and precariousness of information relating to these sources make it uncertain to precisely determine the beginning of the *res judicata* doctrine. At most, one could say that the doctrine of *res judicata* dates back to the third century AD, since the *Digest*, on this topic, refers to Modestinus and Ulpian.[9]

On the other side of the English Channel, the influence of Roman law only became relevant many centuries later. The instability of the Roman occupation caused by British resistance, from the first century AD to their withdrawal in the fifth century, mitigated the influence of the Roman legal system in Great Britain. Only in the sixth century, with the advent of Christianity and, with it, the ecclesiastical courts, did Roman legal doctrines come to the knowledge of British jurists. Nevertheless, it is only with the Norman Conquest, in the eleventh century—notably with the invitation to Lombard Vacarius to teach Roman Law in Oxford—that the Roman legal system spread—and, with it, the doctrine of *res judicata.*[10]

There are, therefore, between 500 and 800 years of parallel traditions regarding *res judicata* in Rome and the British Isles.

Indeed, the need to stabilise judicial decisions in order to provide legal certainty and social peace, the ultimate goal of the Roman doctrine of *res judicata*, had to be met by another means in Great Britain. The space left by the absence of *res judicata* allowed for the development of a parallel doctrine.

The doctrine by which the ancient English ensured the stability of their judicial decisions stemmed from a principle of substantive law called *estoppel.*[11] The *estoppel* is a doctrine of substantive law formed from ethical premises aimed at preventing disloyalty in social relations, similar to the Latin *venire contra factum proprium.* The *estoppel*, like the *venire,* is understood as a general clause of objective good faith that prohibits a subject from behaving contradictorily in a way that harms third parties.[12]

Now, the ancient English began to apply this principle to the process when they noticed, in the procedural behaviour of the parties, manifestations against which they could not subsequently contradict themselves. Thus, their allegations, refutations, evidentiary checks, once they were part of the records (*records*), could not be

[9] Nieva (2006), pp. 30–41.

[10] Cf. Scrutton (1885).

[11] Marinoni (2018), pp. 31–50.

[12] Cf, among all, Cordeiro (2013), pp. 742–751, and Costa (2018), § 74, n. 1–4.

contradicted by them. Hence, the *estoppel by record*. Over time, the English realised that judicial decisions derived from the procedural behaviour of the parties. What they alleged, proved, defended, ended up framing, so to speak, the decision made in the process. The judicial decision, therefore, as a kind of by-product of the procedural behaviour of the parties, could also not be contradicted, as this would represent, reflexively, a contradiction to the behaviour of the parties, prohibited by the *estoppel by record*.

Thus, the parties could not contradict what was established in a judicial decision, not because the judicial decision, in itself, was immutable and indisputable, but because, in doing so, the parties contradicted their own procedural behaviour, which was prohibited by that principle of substantive law, the *estoppel*. From the *estoppel by record* comes the *collateral estoppel*, namely the prohibition of relitigating what has been judicially established.

It was not, properly speaking, a prohibition on the courts, but on the parties. Not a prohibition to decide again what has already been decided, but to litigate what has already been litigated.

Hence, unlike the Roman *res judicata*, in the English *collateral estoppel*, there is no restriction on the claim or the device. The judgement is only indirectly the place of stabilisation. It is so only insofar as it represents a derivation of the procedural behaviour of the parties. This, indeed, is what must be stabilised.

Therefore, it is in a very broad formula that the *collateral estoppel* is born to prevent the parties from reopening discussions about what has been decided. Everything that, in the decision, corresponds to a procedural behaviour of the parties, cannot be questioned again. The stabilisation, therefore, is not limited to the judgement of the main claims being upheld or dismissed, but can reach the logically antecedent issues that the judge comes to resolve when they derive from the parties' allegations. It is for this reason that English law already had a long tradition of recognising the indisputability of issues decided in court when the Romanist doctrine arrived in Great Britain.

Later, with the arrival of *res judicata* and all its adjacent conceptual repertoire, the English (and, especially, the Americans, as future heirs of this legal tradition) began to recognise two areas of indisputability and immutability: one in the main claim—the *claim preclusion*, corresponding to the traditional notion of Roman *res judicata* on the claim/device—and another in the preliminary issues—the *issue preclusions*, corresponding to the *collateral estoppel* (incidental issues resolved when there is a final decision on the merits) and to the *direct estoppel* (incidental issues resolved that prevent the resolution of the merits—such as the prohibition of refiling an action identical to another that, previously, was dismissed for lack of legitimacy).

Indeed, in Anglo-Saxon law, one speaks of *issue preclusion* (preclusion on issue) when a legal controversy appears incidentally to the main claim, as a preliminary issue, and cannot be litigated because it has already been resolved in a previous process. On the other hand, one speaks of *claim preclusion* (preclusion of "merit", in the absence of a better translation for the controversial technical sense of the concept of *claim*), when the main claim cannot be known because it has already been the subject of a decision. judicially adjudicated in a previous case.[13]

2.3 Critique of Mutuality: Subjective Extension of *Res Judicata* on Issues and the *Non-mutual Collateral Estoppel*

As observed, in legal systems inspired by Saxon law, the discussion about the objective limits of *res judicata* causes less difficulty than in Roman-Germanic systems, with a reasonable consensus, due to the effects of the *collateral estoppel* on what is conventionally called *issue preclusion,* that decisions on preliminary issues are also indisputable by the parties.[14]

However, over the years, Roman influence has prevailed in terms of the *subjective* limits of *res judicata*, obscuring for the English the possibility of seeing the prohibition of re-discussion of issues, both main and preliminary, beyond the parties in the process.[15] In other words, like the Romans, the English believed that *res judicata* only produced effects between the parties to the process in which the decision was made.[16] The *collateral estoppel*, therefore, could only apply to prevent the re-discussion of preliminary issues decided in the course of a process if, in the subsequent process, the issue was to be discussed exclusively by the same parties.

However, following a compelling challenge to Roman logic made by Jeremy Bentham in the early decades of the 1800s, the English (and, especially, the Americans) began to question the extension of the *subjective* effects of *res judicata*, starting to consider the possibility of extending its effects to third parties.

---

[13] Cf. Clermont (2016), pp. 1.106–1.122. Cavanagh (2019), pp. 286–295. Hazard and Taruffo (1993), pp. 172–173; 191–193. In this conception, the final judgement of the merit sentence merges, so to speak, the sentence to the whole process, making the resolution on the claim immutable and indisputable. When a preliminary issue is resolved, it is said that the discussion about the resolved incidental controversy is barred to the defeated litigant.

[14] Cf. the text of § 27 of the Restatement (Second) of Judgements, in footnote n. 6, above.

[15] Although the object of the present study is the objective limits of res judicata, the developments of collateral estoppel about its subjective limits prove interesting for three reasons: (i) they demonstrate the unnecessary focus exclusively on the claim made by the parties or on the provision of the sentence that judges it; (ii) they reveal the unnecessary need for the Roman institute of res judicata to meet the need for stabilisation of the judicial decision, it being possible to construct a different solution; and (iii) they highlight the need to balance security and freedom to ensure an adequate extension to res judicata, cf. above Sect. 3.2, the balance between material security and procedural freedom as a criterion for defining the objective limits of res judicata. It is with this emphasis that the next lines will be discussed.

[16] The requirements for the prohibition of the re-discussion of the decided issue were therefore mutuality (collateral estoppel only prevents re-discussion between the same parties) or privity (the successors of the parties in the litigious object were also prohibited from re-discussing the previous decision).

Bentham's reasoning reveals the Saxon pragmatism regarding *res judicata*, extremely focused on ensuring the right of participation of those who suffer the effects of the judicial decision and, at the same time, not exceeding this right—that is, providing a broad expansion of the judicial decision, as long as the right to action is ensured, increasing the efficiency of the courts and the economy of the process.

In short, according to this reasoning, every citizen should be protected against *res judicata* formed in a process in which they did not have the opportunity to influence the conviction of the court formed. But, if the citizen had this opportunity, it makes no sense to prevent *res judicata* from producing its effects against this citizen, simply because the opposing party did not participate in the previous process.[17] Now, the restriction of the *collateral estoppel* to the parties of the process would produce a *non sense*: while this third party would be prevented from alleging the prohibition of re-discussion of the issue already decided in the previous process to the detriment of his counterparty, the one who was part of the process, and succumbed, would have a new chance to discuss a legal relationship on which the State-Judge has already definitively pronounced in another process. Such a benefit, however, was of dubious legitimacy, as it would allow the citizen to re-discuss an issue for whose resolution he had already contributed.

Not only in doctrine but also in jurisprudence, there were already beginning to appear flexibilities to the rule of mutuality. The notorious case, in jurisprudence, was that of the driver who, driving a vehicle of a third party, gets involved in a car accident. If the driver responded to an action and was acquitted for having been considered absent his civil liability for the case (absence of fault or causal link, for example), the author of the action would be *estopped* from relitigating about the civil liability of the driver, using the subterfuge of merely redirecting the action against the third owner of the vehicle.[18]

This is a glaring demonstration of the objectivity of the *collateral estoppel*: once the material legal issue on which a party seeks judicial protection is resolved, it is not allowed to relitigate it, even with another request and against another party.

But the argument used by the judges until then was that the car accident case did not represent the overcoming, but an exception to the rule of mutuality.

[17] *"There is reason for a saying that a man shall not lose his cause in consequence of the verdict given in a former proceeding to which he was not a party; but there is no reason whatever for saying that he shall not lose his cause in consequence of a verdict in a proceeding to which he was a party, merely because his adversary was not."* Bentham (1843), p. 171.

[18] Note, Res Judicata - mutuality of estoppel and privity rules in automobile negligence field. New York University Law Quarterly Review, n. 18, 1941, p. 565 et seq. *apud* Marinoni (2018), p. 76.

2.3.1 Bernhard v. Bank of America

of the *collateral estoppel,* admitting it when invoked by a third party, was given in the case *Bernhard v. Bank of America National Trust & Savings Assoc.*[19]

Charles Cook was the caretaker of an elderly woman, named Clara Sather. Due to her frail health, Mrs. Sather authorised the bank to make financial transactions in her name when ordered jointly by her doctor and her caretaker, Mr. Cook. Later, Cook opened an account in the name of "Clara Sather *by* Charles O. Cook" at San Dimas Bank, possibly to facilitate transactions. In other words, it was an account where the resources were supposedly Mrs. Sather's, but could be moved by Mr. Cook. At a certain point, Mrs. Sather went to the bank where she kept the account whose joint movement by the doctor and the caretaker was authorised and, accompanied by these two gentlemen, authorised the transfer of a substantial amount to this account that Mr. Cook had opened to operate on behalf of Mrs. Sather, at the San Dimas Bank. Later, Mr. Cook transferred the money from that account to an account opened in his name.

That same year, Mrs. Sather passed away and Cook was appointed executor of the estate left by the deceased. In the statements made by Cook, he requested that those values then transferred to his account be excluded from Mrs. Sather's estate, arguing that it was a gift from her to him. The beneficiaries of the inheritance, among whom was Mrs. Helen Bernhard, contested, claiming that the values should be part of the estate. After the instruction, the probate judge decided that the value had been given to Mr. Cook as a gift, and not to be used for the administration of the needs of the deceased, accepting Mr. Cook's request, and therefore, rejecting the request of Mrs. Bernhard.

Therefore, in the probate process of Mrs. Sather's assets, it was decided, incidentally, that the values received by Cook did not form part of the estate.

Subsequently, Mrs. Bernhard filed a lawsuit against the Bank of America (here is the case *Bernhard v. Bank of America),* successor of San Dimas Bank, claiming reimbursement to the estate of the values raised by Cook.

In its defence, the bank argued that the issue had already been decided by the probate judge, in the previous action, which declared that the value raised by Cook was a gift given by Mrs. Sather, invoking the authority of that *res judicata* to prevent re-litigation on the same issue.

The Court accepted the bank's claim and the Supreme Court of California confirmed this decision, stating that, although the Bank of America had not been part of the probate process, where Mrs. Bernhard's request had already been rejected, this would not be relevant, as "when a party, although appearing in two processes with different qualities, is in fact litigating the same right, the decision in one prevents it in the other". After all, although the bank, which had raised the *collateral estoppel* in its defence, had not been part of the previous process, "why a party that was not bound by a previous action should be prevented from alleging it as *res judicata*

[19] L. A. No. 18057. In Bank. Mar. 6, 1942.

against a party that was bound by it is hard to understand. (...) Most courts have, in fact, arrived at the same result, recognising a broad exception to the requirements of *mutuality* and *privity*, namely, that they are not necessary when the liability of the defendant claiming the exception of *res judicata* is dependent or derived from the liability of someone who was exonerated in a previous action filed by the same plaintiff based on the same facts".

And after exposing cases usually accepted in jurisprudence for overcoming mutuality, notably the case of the aforementioned car accident, the Court affirmed that "the *estoppel* is not mutual, in the sense that the party claiming the exception, for not having been a party or substituted it in relation to the object of the dispute in the previous action, would not be bound by it if it had been decided otherwise. The cases justify this exception with the argument that it would be unfair to allow someone who had their day in Court to reopen identical issues just by changing adversaries". And concluded, establishing true doctrinal precedent: "to determine the validity of a claim of *res judicata*, three questions are pertinent: Was the issue decided in the previous sentence identical to the one presented in the action in question? Was there a final judgment on the merits? Was the party against whom the exception is claimed a party or did it substitute it in the object of the dispute in the previous adjudication?"

As can be seen, the precedent of *Bernhard* reveals a doctrine according to which *res judicata* should apply with broad subjective and objective scope, whenever an issue resolved in a final judgement is litigated again by a party harmed in the previous decision.[20] And note that the main issue proposed in *Bernhard* was resolved, in the previous probate process, incidentally. That is, the main issue in the case *Bernhard* was prejudicial in the probate action. And, even so, its resolution prevented (*estopped*) Mrs. Bernhard from discussing it again. Thus, the *collateral estoppel* produced in the probate action barred the discussion of the entire cause (*claim*) in *Bernhard*, despite the previous resolution having occurred only incidentally (*issue*).

2.3.2 *Blonder-Tongue v. University of Illinois: The So-Called Defensive Non-Mutual Collateral Estoppel*

Although the case *Bernhard* did not reach the Supreme Court of the United States of America, the doctrine enshrined in it was confirmed almost thirty years later in the judgement of *Blonder-Tongue Labs., Inc. v. University of Ill. Foundation*,[21]

---

[20] Such an extension of the effects of res judicata generated great doctrinal discussion. Especially—but not only—because of the overcoming of mutuality. For example: Currie (1957) and Waggoner (1993).

[21] 402 U.S. 313 (1971).

when, for the first time, the controversy regarding the necessity or not of *privity and mutuality* reached that Supreme Court.

In the case, the University of Illinois had lost a previous action in which it claimed compensation for patent infringement. In this previous action, the Court deemed the patent claimed by the University to be invalid. Subsequently, the University claimed new compensation for the infringement of the same patent, this time against a third party, the Blonder-Tongue laboratory. The defendant defended themselves by arguing that the University was *estopped* from litigating about the validity of the plaintiff's patent, due to the *res judicata* produced in the previous action, which was ultimately accepted by the Supreme Court of the United States.

Note that, unlike in *Bernhard*, in *Blonder-Tongue,* the *collateral estoppel* presented itself in the form of *issue preclusion* in both actions: the validity of the patent was a preliminary issue to the main claim for compensation in both cases. The declaration of the patent's invalidity in the first action, which resulted in the dismissal of the claim, prevented its re-litigation in the second action, also as a preliminary issue.

It is immediately apparent that the criterion for preventing the re-litigation of a legal issue in the American system has nothing to do with the parties, nor with the claim or the cause of action. Instead of the so-called "triple identity", the criterion for determining the existence or non-existence of *res judicata* is the substantive legal relationship discussed.[22] In other words, once a decision has been made on the invalidity of patent "X" invoked by party "Y" in a process with the fundamental guarantees of the parties (especially the disadvantaged party), it matters little in what procedural context this issue is subsequently raised (whether "Y" appears as plaintiff or defendant, whoever the counterparty may be, whatever the claim or cause of action), it is not possible to re-litigate it.

Indeed, although the Supreme Court had recognised, in *Blonder-Tongue*, that the rule of mutuality of *collateral estoppel* was *out of place*, it limited its claim to the defendant who intended to use the *collateral estoppel* in their defence (*defensive nonmutual collateral estoppel*).

2.3.3 *Parklane v. Shore: The So-Called Offensive Non-Mutual Collateral Estoppel*

There is another precedent from that Court that will not be discussed in this study, either due to the well-founded criticisms and deep suspicion on the part of American proceduralists, or because it has little relevance to the issue of the *objective* limits of *res judicata*, focusing primarily on the *subjective.* This precedent will only be

[22] This argument is more fully set out below, in Sect. 3.1.3.1: "Critical interval: how this binomial makes it difficult to visualise the extension of the objective limits of res judicata. First outline on the objective limits of res judicata: triple identity or decision on substantive legal relationship?"

mentioned to acknowledge and illustrate that, even in the Anglo-Saxon system, the study of the limits of *res judicata* proves to be, in fact, challenging.

In *Parklane Hosiery Co., Inc. v. Shore*,[23] Shore held shares in a securities market managed by Parklane Co. After suffering a significant financial loss, Shore filed a lawsuit against Parklane claiming compensation, alleging that Parklane had provided false information, violating federal law on the management of the financial assets it held. It was a *class action* in which Shore was the representative and, as such, had a protracted course.

While Shore's case was ongoing, the *U. S. Security in Exchange Commission* (SEC)[24] identified that Parklane was about to provide information it believed to be false, posing a risk to the market, and filed a lawsuit against Parklane alleging that it had already committed the same violation of federal law (as alleged by Shore) and was about to repeat it, hence it sought an *injunction* to prevent such illicit repetition.

This second action, filed by the SEC, was judged to be valid, with the Court recognising that Parklane had indeed provided false information and violated federal law, granting the *injunction*.

Realising that the issue resolved in this action was identical to that litigated in his *class action,* Shore requested a partial summary judgement, arguing that Parklane could not re-litigate the issue regarding the falsity of the information provided. He was invoking a new type, the *offensive non-mutual collateral estoppel.*

Initially, the District Court did not accept Shore's request, on the grounds that, unlike the action filed by the SEC, the jurisdiction in the *class action* was with the Jury (Seventh Amendment). The State Court dismissed the argument of jurisdiction, which it considered to be secondary to the prohibition of re-litigating the same issue, which was confirmed by the Supreme Court of the United States, according to which the provision of the jury would not guarantee a better opportunity to exercise the right to a fair trial and full defence—these, indeed, relevant elements to recognise the possibility of preventing Parklane from re-litigating about the illegality of its statements to the market.

However, in declaring that the *non-mutual collateral estoppel* does not it is restricted to the defendant's defence, and can be claimed by the plaintiff to prevent the re-discussion of an issue that the defendant could raise in his defence. The Supreme Court recognised that this is not a situation that applies to all cases, leaving a wide margin of discretion to the courts to decide on its application.[25]

---

[23] 439 U.S. 322 (1979).

[24] National administrative authority with competence for regulation and supervision of securities, similar to the Securities Commissions of Brazil and Portugal. Cf. https://www.sec.gov/.

[25] "We conclude that the best way to deal with these problems [that may not recommend the offensive collateral estoppel] is not to prohibit the offensive collateral estoppel, but to grant the Courts broad discretion to decide when it should be applied." Parklane Hosiery Co., Inc. v. Shore, 439 U.S. 322 (1979).

Although *Parklane* is the subject of significant and well-founded doctrinal criticisms,[26] the same rationale used in *Blonder-Tongue* is upheld here by the *Justices,* which is relevant for understanding the phenomenon of *collateral estoppel* in relation to the objective of this chapter: to expand the horizons of procedural law based on *res judicata* and to envisage the reasonableness of extending *res judicata* to decisions on preliminary issues, provided certain requirements are met.

According to the Court, "in light of the serious allegations made by the SEC against the appellants [in the previous action], as well as the likely risk of subsequent private actions that typically follow a judgement favourable to the Government, the appellants [Parklane] had every incentive to litigate the SEC action fully and vigorously. (...) Since the appellants had a full and fair opportunity to litigate in the action brought by the SEC, the contemporary understanding of *collateral estoppel* inevitably leads to the conclusion that the appellants are *collaterally estopped* from litigating the issue of whether the 'information' (*proxy statement*) presented by Parklane and Seomekh was materially false and misleading".

2.4 Restatement (Second) of Judgements: The Requirements of Non-Mutual Collateral Estoppel, Its Influence on the Brazilian CPC of 2015 and the Possibilities in Portugal

As can be seen from the above precedents, the American "*res judicata*" has always encompassed *claim preclusion* and *issue preclusion* with the same intensity. But the breaking of mutuality forced American jurists to delineate more precisely the limits of *collateral estoppel,* which ended up, with a precipitous basis in the above precedents, being established in §§ 26 to 28 of the *Restatement (Second) of Judgements.* This was a useful occasion to understand, with reasonable certainty, how far *collateral estoppel* goes. According to the compiled text, there are three requirements for the application of *non-mutual defensive collateral estoppel:* (i) that the issue is concretely identical (not just sufficiently similar), (ii) that there was a final judgement on the merits, and (iii) that the person who is intended to be prohibited from

[26] The crux of the criticism pertains to mass conflicts. When the legal phenomenon generating controversies transcends heterogeneous individuality, several autonomous individual actions based on the same (homogeneous) interests may repeat. In this case, the offensive use of collateral estoppel diminishes the effectiveness of judicial protection, as it inhibits the proposition of joint demands insofar as, if an action is judged to be successful, all future litigants benefit; but, in case of failure, there is no harm to litigants who did not participate (res judicata secundum eventum litis). The strategy called "wait and see" harms the rationality of justice distribution and the coherence of law, as even if the first thirty-nine actions are unfavourable to the plaintiffs, res judicata could benefit all subsequent litigants who did not participate—or waited—due to the decision rendered in the fortieth action. Cf. Currie (1957), Marinoni (2018), p. 90 and Kempkes (1980).

re-discussing had been a party in the process in which the decision was made, with a *full and fair opportunity* to participate.[27]

The similarity of these requirements with those of *res judicata* on preliminary issues, erected in §§ 1 and 2 of art. 503 of the Brazilian CPC, is striking.

According to Brazilian legislation, for a preliminary issue to have "force of law", it needs: (i) to be expressly decided, even if incidentally, and provided that (ii) its resolution depends on the judgement of the merits, (iii) "there has been prior and effective contradiction, not applying in the case of default", (iv) the court is competent and (v) there have been no "evidentiary restrictions or limitations to cognition that prevent the deepening of the analysis of the preliminary issue".

In summary, a preliminary issue can be covered by *res judicata* if it is effectively and fully litigated and expressly decided, without any evidentiary, allegatory, or cognitive limitation, by a competent judge.

Now, the three American precedents cited above (*Bernhard, Blonder-Tongue,* and *Parklane*) would pass the test of Brazilian legislation, with ease (except Parklane, perhaps, due to the competence of the jury for the *class action*).

It can be seen, therefore, that the Brazilian *res judicata* on preliminary issues has a broad scope, quite similar to that of the American *issue preclusion/collateral estoppel*.

But it was not always like this.

In the Code of Civil Procedure of Brazil of 1973, prior to the currently in force, the system was that of the so-called "incidental declaratory action". Through an incidental request, the party expands the object on which jurisdiction should be provided so that the judge declares, with the force of *res judicata*, the existence or non-existence of a legal relationship on which the merits of the case depend.

According to the system of arts. 5, 325, and 470 of the Brazilian CPC of 1973, if the "right that constitutes the basis of the request" was contested by the defendant, or if a "litigious legal relationship of whose existence or "non-existence depends on the judgement of the dispute", the interested party could request, within a certain period, that the judge incidentally declare the right over this controversy. Only in this case, through the initiation of a procedural incident, could a prejudicial issue be resolved with the force of *res judicata*.

The system is similar to that provided for in art. 91, no. 2, of the Portuguese CPC, according to which the "decision of the issues and incidents raised does not, however, constitute *res judicata* outside the respective process, except if one of the parties requests the judgement with this scope and the court is competent from an international point of view and in terms of the subject matter and hierarchy".

Just like the previous Brazilian model, for a prejudicial issue to be resolved with the force of *res judicata*, the Portuguese model requires the party to explicitly postulate that the decisions made to resolve such issues are produced with the force of *res judicata*.

[27] Marinoni (2018), pp. 75–93; Marinoni (2016), § 10.

Imagine how this system would work, for example, in the case *Blonder-Tongue*, described above: the University of Illinois filed a lawsuit seeking compensation from a company for patent infringement, which is dismissed as the patent raised by the plaintiff was considered invalid; subsequently, the same University files a new action against Blonder-Tongue, again claiming compensation for infringement of the same patent, previously declared incidentally invalid in the previous process.

If such action were filed under Portuguese law, it would be possible for the second action to be upheld—or, at least, that the patent deemed invalid against the first defendant would be considered valid in the action brought against Blonder-Tongue, since, under the terms of art. 91, no. 2, the resolution regarding the validity of the patent would only constitute *res judicata* if it was expressly requested by one of the parties. Both the procedural behaviour of the parties and the objective fact that the validity of the patent was effectively litigated and decided would not be sufficient to prevent the issue from being discussed again—and, even, contradicted.

It is not being asserted that the American model should be imported thoughtlessly to Portugal, nor that it has been by Brazil, but that it can be adapted where it is compatible with the Roman-Germanic systems. For example, the competence of the judge, considered irrelevant by the *Supreme Court* in *Parklane*, is considered fundamental in the new Brazilian model.[28]

This serves as an example to demonstrate that a model can be *incorporated with adaptations*. But it also serves, as, indeed, is hoped, this entire chapter, to desensitize the operator of the Roman-Germanic legal system and desacralize the objective limitation of *res judicata* to the judgement's device, expanding its horizons and helping to perceive the same phenomenon from a different perspective, as well as that it is possible—and, perhaps, even more logical, reasonable, and safe—to extend the effects of *res judicata* to the decision on the issue, instead of fumbling in the dark in search of the limits of the authority of *res judicata*, trying to intuit, without secure criteria, in which cases it is possible to attribute effects of *res judicata* to the "grounds".

And that is what, in the next chapter, we intend to analyse: what are, specifically, the grounds to which the authority of *res judicata* can be attributed, based on which criteria and according to which values.

But first, a final practical consideration. The Brazilian solution was to change the statute, with a new Code of Civil Procedure in 2015. In the Portuguese case, if the statute is not changed—that is, keeping in force art. 91, no. 2, of the CPC, the alternative could be the updating of this provision through its interpretation in conformity with the Constitution.

---

[28] Moreira (1967), p. 92. On the following page, Barbosa Moreira notes that not only the jurisdiction of the court would be fundamental to assess the possibility of extending res judicata to the resolution of a preliminary issue, but also the procedure. An example is the impossibility of, in a reivindicatory action, achieving res judicata for the decision that recognises the defendant's quiet and peaceful possession for a period longer than that of extraordinary usucaption, as mentioned in Sect. 4.2 of this work.

That is to say, the technique of declaring unconstitutionality without text reduction, advocated, originally, in the Federal Constitutional Court of Germany, to preserve a legal text that should not be declared null when it can be interpreted in accordance with the Constitution.[29] From this technique, it will be possible to attribute normative efficacy to this provision in accordance with the constitutional values that govern the institute of *res judicata*, as, finally, will also be demonstrated in the next chapter.

After all, the *telos* of art. 91, no. 2, is to point to a controversial issue about which one of the parties wishes to litigate and obtain a decision with the force of *res judicata*. Now, if what matters is the observance of procedural guarantees and the express decision on the issue, then, having this, there is no need to require that the party explicitly postulate that such a decision be covered by *res judicata*. Such a requirement, by leaving prejudicial issues exposed that could have been stabilised (because they were effectively litigated and expressly decided), but, due to lack of express request, were not, exposes the deficient protection of the principle of legal certainty and the excessive protection of procedural freedom.

But all this will be clarified in the next chapter.

References

Baini GM (2024a) Extensão dos efeitos objetivos da coisa julgada anglo-saxônica: o collateral estoppel. Revista Eletrônica Consultor Jurídico. https://www.conjur.com.br/2024-jan-25/extensao-dos-efeitos-objetivos-da-coisa-julgada-anglo-saxonica-o-collateral-estoppel. Acessed 06 de August de 2025

Baini GM (2024b) Extensão dos efeitos objetivos da coisa julgada anglo-saxônica (parte 2). Revista Eletrônica Consultor Jurídico. https://www.conjur.com.br/2024-jan-25/extensao-dos-efeitos-objetivos-da-coisa-julgada-anglo-saxonica-o-collateral-estoppel. Acessed 06 de August de 2025

Bentham J (1843) Rationale of judicial evidence. In: Bentham J (ed) The works of Jeremy Bentham, vol VII. Simpkin, Marshall & Co., Edinburgh

Bersier N et al (2022) Common law - civil law – the great divide? Springer, Chaim

Calabresi G (1982) A common law for the age of statutes. Harvard Univ. Press, Cambridge

Canotilho JJG (2003) Direito constitucional e teoria da constituição. Almedina, Coimbra

Cavanagh ED (2019) Offensive non-mutual issue preclusion revisited. Rev Litig 38(3):281–331. https://scholarship.law.stjohns.edu/faculty_publications. Accessed 06 Aug 2025

Clermont KM (2016) Res Judicata as requisite for justice. Rutgers Univ Law Rev 68:1.067–1.139

Cordeiro AM (2013) Da boa-fé no direito civil. Almedina, Coimbra

Costa JM (2018) A boa-fé no direito privado. Saraiva, São Paulo

Currie B (1957) Mutuality of collateral estoppel: limits of the Bernhard doctrine. Stanford Law Rev 9(2):281–322

David R (2002) Os grandes sistemas do direito contemporâneo. Martins Fontes, São Paulo

Freitas JL (2019) Um polvo chamado autoridade do caso julgado. Revista da Ordem dos Advogados 79(3–4):691–722

[29] On all, cf. Hesse (1983), Medeiros (1999), p. 317, Mendes (1998), p. 270, Canotilho (2003), p. 1.226.

Hazard GC Jr, Taruffo M (1993) American Civil Procedure - an introduction. Yale University Press, New Haven/London

Hesse K (1983) La interpretación constitucional. In: Hesse K (ed) Escritos de derecho constitucional. Centro de Estudios Constitucionales, Madrid

Kempkes B (1980) Issue preclusion: Parklane Hosiery Co. v. Shore, revisited. Drake Law Rev 31(1):111–130

MacCormick N, Summers B (1991) Interpreting statutes – a comparative study. Routledge, London and New York

MacCormick N et al (1997) Interpreting precedents – a comparative study. Routledge, London and New York

Marinoni LG (2016) Coisa julgada sobre questão, inclusive em benefício de terceiro. Revista de Processo 259:97–116

Marinoni LG (2018) Coisa julgada sobre questão. Revista dos Tribunais, São Paulo

Medeiros R (1999) A decisão de inconstitucionalidade. Univ. Católica, Lisboa

Mendes GF (1998) Jurisdição constitucional: o controle abstrato de normas no Brasil e na Alemanha. Saraiva, São Paulo

Moreira JCB (1967) Questões prejudiciais e coisa julgada. 1967. PhD Thesis (Livre-docência in Judiciary Law), Law School at Federal University of Rio de Janeiro

Nieva JF (2006) La cosa juzgada. Atelier, Barcelona

Scrutton TE (1885) The influence of the Roman Law on the Law of England. Cambridge University Press, Cambridge

Waggoner MJ (1993) Fifty years of Bernhard v. Bank of America is enough: collateral estoppel should require mutuality but res judicata should not. Rev Litig 12:391. https://scholar.law.colorado.edu/faculty-articles/821. Accessed 08 Aug 2025

Chapter 3
The Roman-Germanic Problems: In Search of the Fundamental Legal Conformation of the Right to *Res Judicata*

As stated in the introduction, the subject of this study is the extension of the effects of *res judicata* to decisions on preliminary issues. The hypothesis here is that, provided certain requirements are met, such an extension gives appropriate treatment to *res judicata*, attributing to it appropriate legal effects to achieve its purpose: to stabilise judicial decisions, without neglecting the need for flexibility, advocating, so to speak, an optimal point of social peace.

To test this hypothesis, it is necessary, first of all, to "clear the field". Therefore, we will establish some concepts that can contribute to the clarification of the controversies that will be addressed.

3.1 Some Basic and Useful Definitions

One of the great challenges for scientific dialogue to advance in the development of *res judicata* is the conceptual vocabulary. There are endless discussions about the words that designate what we want to represent, both in law and in doctrine. Effects, efficacy, force, quality, or authority of the judgement (or of *res judicata*), efficacy or preclusive effect of *res judicata* (or of the judgement), indisputability, immutability, imperativeness, to name just a few examples of concepts about which there is no unanimously accepted content.

The following will exclusively address some basic definitions relevant for analysing the hypothesis of this study, consciously leaving out various other conceptual controversies that are admittedly relevant for other purposes.

G. M. Baini, *Objective Limits of Res Judicata*, SpringerBriefs in Law,
https://doi.org/10.1007/978-3-032-07485-0_3

3.1.1 *Adjudicated Case,* Res Judicata*, and Preclusion*

The need for stabilisation of judicial decisions is felt, as mentioned in the introduction, from prehistoric peoples to today, in almost all minimally civilised legal systems. It is, therefore, a practically universal legal value.[1]

However, the way this value is concretised internally in each legal system is extremely varied. It is certain that the distinction between *res judicata* and case adjudicated, translations of the Latin expression *res judicata* chosen, respectively, in Brazil[2] and Portugal, goes far beyond the names. The institutes of Brazilian *res judicata* and Portuguese case adjudicated have distinctions within the legal system and doctrinal discussion of each of the corresponding countries—as, indeed, occurs in all legal systems, which colour their own legal institutes that, due to their similarity, partially transcend national borders and are represented by similar names, such as the *cosa judicatta* Italian, the *cosa juzgada* Spanish, and the *chose jugée* French, to name three significant examples.

Nevertheless, the term "res judicata", in this study, will mean what both institutes—the Brazilian and the Portuguese—have in common: namely, the prohibition of re-discussion about what has been decided, in a prohibitive aspect (or, on the other side of the coin, the need to observe what has been decided, in an imposing aspect).[3] This is what can most fundamentally be said about *res judicata* and case adjudicated (and, probably, about the *cosa judicatta*, the *cosa juzgada,* and the *chose jugée*). In this study, therefore, *res judicata* will be called the stabilisation of the judicial decision[4] aimed at social peace.

This stabilisation occurs through the prohibition of re-discussion about what has been decided. Or, in other words, which is to say the same thing: by imposing observance (*rectius:* the binding) of judges and parties to what has been decided.[5] The objective extension of res judicata, in this sense, would concern its material limits: what, in a judicial decision, binds and cannot be re-discussed?

---

[1] Clermont (2016), pp. 1.071–1.078.

[2] As will be seen later, the Introduction to the Norms in Brazilian Law designates "res judicata" and "adjudicated case" as synonyms. The Brazilian legal tradition, however, has consecrated the first term in place of the second.

[3] Perhaps a good designation for this positive aspect would be "bindingness", or, as Rui Pinto tempers, "mandatory force". By naming the prohibition of rediscussion "negative effect", and the imposition of observance "positive effect", the author rightly observes that these are "two sides of the special quality of the judicial decision that has become final, under the terms of article 628: the 'mandatory force' of the judicial decision within the process (cf. article 620) and outside it, when it judges on the merits (cf. article 619)." Pinto (2018a), pp. 152–153.

[4] José Carlos Barbosa Moreira (2011) highlights the "multiplicity of conceptualisations" and the "equivocality of the very concept from which the elaborations of the doctrinarians develop" (p. 91), trying to reduce them to what he identified as the essentially practical function of res judicata: "to ensure stability to the judicial protection provided by the State." Moreira (2011), p. 93.

[5] Surely influenced by the text of arts. 619 and 620 of their Code of Civil Procedure, the portuguese lawyers often use the expression "mandatory force", assimilated to the German term to designate res judicata: RechtsKraft.

We will deal with *res judicata*, therefore, from the perspective of process theory: more as a general value conceptually defined here than, properly, as a codified institute, with all its meticulous contours.[6] This is because, if the object of this study is to assess the possibility of *res judicata* (the prohibition and the binding) extending to decisions on preliminary issues, then there is no need to restrict its contours to some codified and/or already developed in doctrine.

It is possible to distinguish this notion of *res judicata* from another notion linked to it: preclusion. In the classic Chiovenda definition, preclusion is "the loss, extinction or consummation of a procedural faculty".[7]

The relationship between preclusion and *res judicata* lies in the fact that both have a stabilising function. The former, however, is procedural: it aims to stabilise the practice of procedural acts by ensuring that, once their content is stabilised, the next act can be performed, and thus, the process can advance. The latter, in the sense adopted here, is of a material order: it ensures the stability of the *content* of what has been decided. In a way, *res judicata* derives from a preclusion, the know, about the extinction of the procedural faculty to discuss the disputed object.

3.1.2 *Formal* Res Judicata *and Substantive* Res Judicata

The understanding of *res judicata* as a consequence of a preclusion on the disputed object can be found in art. 502 of the Brazilian CPC which states: "Substantive res judicata is the authority that makes the decision on the merits unchangeable and indisputable, no longer subject to appeal". If no further appeal is possible, this means that the procedural faculty to discuss the disputed object resolved in the decision is extinguished. The party is precluded from such faculty and the decision on the merits becomes, therefore, unchangeable and indisputable. The combination of these two qualities generates, in the legal sense, the authority called substantive *res judicata material.*

On the other hand, art. 6, § 3, of the Introduction to the Norms in Brazilian Law[8] (former "Introduction to the Civil Code") establishes that "Res judicata or adjudicated case is the judicial decision from which no further appeal is possible". This second definition, more restricted, as it is only linked to the moment when *res judicata* is formed and not properly to its substantive content, is traditionally associated with what the Luso-Brazilian doctrine calls formal res judicata *formal.*[9]

[6] Some positive elements may be highlighted, here and there, more with the aim of illustrating the propositions produced and the construction of a "pure" conception of res judicata.

[7] Accordind to Sousa (2017), p. 149, refering to Giuseppe Chiovenda's Essays on civil procedural law (1993). v. III, pp. 232 and 233, and. v. II, p. 414 and ss.

[8] The Introduction to the Norms in Brazilian Law (Decree-Law No. 4,657/1942) is the statute that sets forth the rules governing the manner in which laws are to be applied within the Brazilian legal system.

[9] For example: Oliveira and Mitidiero (2012), p. 273. Mendes (1963), p. 459.

For this doctrine, formal *res judicata* would refer to the insusceptibility of re-discussion of what was decided within the process, a phenomenon of endoprocessual incontestability.[10] The only utility of this classification is to explain the res judicata that ends the process, without necessarily ending the material dispute. That is, even if the merits of the request are not examined (or there is an acquittal of instance, in Portuguese procedural law), there will be formal *res judicata*. Strictly speaking, the formal *res judicata* results from the preclusion that is also called "trânsito em julgado" (final and unappealable judgement).[11]

Therefore, the preclusion resulting from the unappealability of the sentence (formal res judicata, art. 6, § 3, of the LINDB) produces an authority that makes it unchangeable and indisputable (substantive res judicata, art. 502 of the Brazilian CPC) when the merits of the request are examined (i.e., when there is something to make unchangeable and indisputable).

While Brazilian legislation limits itself to expressly defining the substantive *res judicata* (at least nominally expressing the institute), the Portuguese CPC expressly provides, in art. 620, the "formal adjudicated case", establishing, in its number 1, that "The sentences and the orders that fall solely on the procedural relationship have binding force within the process". This is intended to exclude the possibility of a decision that does not concern the material relationship discussed within the process producing effects outside of it—that is, to prevent a merely procedural decision from binding the judges and the parties in a process different from the one in which it was pronounced. The justification is obvious: if the preclusion is procedural, then it concerns only that process in which it was produced. But, on the other hand, the formal adjudicated case imposes this binding within the process, preventing that this procedural issue be discussed again—thus stabilising it.[12]

Then, art. 619 of the Portuguese CPC reveals that "Once the sentence has been finalised (...) that decides on the merits of the case, the decision on the disputed material relationship becomes binding within the process and outside of it (...)". Indeed, unlike the formal adjudicated case, which only binds within the process, the sentence that decides on the merits of the case, judging the disputed material relationship, has binding force within and outside the process. Clearly, this is a concept entirely similar to the Brazilian legal definition of substantive res judicata.[13]

As can be seen at this point, despite the relevance of the distinction between formal and substantive *res judicata* (and between formal and substantive adjudicated case), for the purposes of what is intended to be developed in this study, there

---

[10] Marinoni and Arenhart (2011), p. 632. Freitas (2019), p. 692, textually in footnote n. 3.

[11] Marinoni et al. (2019), p. 637.

[12] Freitas and Alexandre (2015), pp. 752 and ss.

[13] The terms used by Brazilian and Portuguese laws to establish the stability of the content of a judicial decision may be relevant. To say that a *merit decision* is endowed with an *authority* that makes its content *immutable and indisputable* may not exactly correspond, in linguistic-philosophical terms, to what is asserted when it is established that the *decision on the disputed material relationship* becomes *binding* in other processes. This is an example of how the codified institution can present nuances that will not be discussed in this monograph.

is, strictly speaking, only one *res judicata*: the attributes that are added to the sentence, after its final and unappealable judgement,[14] that make unchangeable and indisputable what the judge decides. These are these attributes that stabilise the content of what was decided, prohibiting its re-discussion and binding the parties and judges to its content about the disputed object.

What is usually called formal *res judicata* is, after all, a kind of preclusion, the stabilisation of the judicial decision within the process, making the decision indisputable and unchangeable among the parties that litigate—the last temporal preclusion of the process.[15]

3.1.3 Authority of the Adjudicated Case and Exception of the Adjudicated Case: The Problem of Identity Between Two Causes

An important distinction among Portuguese proceduralists is made between the so-called "authority of the adjudicated case" and "exception of the adjudicated case".[16]

This distinction may be useful in the present study because it may prove to be, as it is intended to show later, insufficiently sustainable or, at most, dispensable. More than that, such distinction may hinder the visualisation of the extension of *res judicata* to the resolution on preliminary issues. This is because it marks the difference between the two sides of the same coin, according to the definition of *res judicata* proceeded in Sect. 2.1.1 above: to prevent the re-discussion of the same controversy already decided (prohibitive face of the coin of *res judicata*), the exception of the adjudicated case is instrumentalised; to impose the controversy already decided in another process (impositive face of the coin of res judicata) the authority of the adjudicated case is instrumentalised.

---

[14] Any discussion about the binding force of the sentence before the final judgement is excluded, simply because it is irrelevant for the purposes intended in this research. See the work of Antonio do Passo Cabral on the topic. For example, in: "Procedural stabilities as a category incorporated into the CPC system." In: Didier Jr. and Cabral (2018). Also excluded is any discussion about whether res judicata is an attribute, quality or efficacy, and whether it affects the sentence or just the effects of the sentence.

[15] Marinoni et al. (2019), pp. 636–637. Long before, Celso Agrícola Barbi considered the formal res judicata to be a "concept that has become useless, and only capable of generating confusion", since its absorption by preclusion is fully possible. See Barbi, C. A. On preclusion in civil procedure. Forensic Review, v. 158, pp. 62–63, cited by Moreira (1967), p. 62. In the same sense see Cabral (2021), chapter 4.1.4.3—"For the end of the difference between preclusion, formal res judicata and substantive res judicata".

[16] On all, see Pinto (2018a), Pinto (2018b), pp. 185–186 and note to article 581. Freitas and Alexandre (2015), pp. 599–600, 754–757; Sousa (1983), pp. 125–140.

In other words, authority and exception would be the tools through which the positive and negative aspects of the *res judicata* are operationalised, respectively.[17]

The element of this binomial that can complicate the understanding of the hypothesis discussed in this paper is the concept of identity between the two disputes. What makes one judicial pronouncement identical to another?

When invoking the exception of *res judicata*, the Portuguese CPC requires the so-called triple identity (parties, claim, and cause of action). However, when there is a need to discuss the effects of *res judicata* on an action where the identity of the three elements is not present, it is common to speak of the authority of *res judicata*. But, after all, if there is no triple identity between two cases, why would there be a need to discuss the effects of the *res judicata* produced in one lawsuit, in another that, in theory, would be distinct? This simple question already reveals that the identity between two cases required by the Portuguese CPC (identity of parties, claim, and cause of action) is inadequate to define the extent of the effects of *res judicata*.

It is important to note that the requirement of triple identity and the conceptualisation of each of the three elements come directly from the genius of the legislator, not being a doctrinal creation.[18] What the doctrine did, by distinguishing the authority from the exception (or rather, by creating the figure of the authority of res judicata), was to try to create an alternative to impose the "binding force" of the decision on the disputed material relationship even when the triple identity is not present, which authorises the instrumentalisation of the exception of *res judicata*.

The uniformity of the doctrine on the distinctions between authority and exception, incidentally, should result from the relative clarity of the legal text in this regard. And, considering such uniformity, the lessons of Rui Pinto will be taken as clear by all.

In Portugal, the exception of *res judicata* expresses the Latin maxim *non bis in idem,* as it presupposes a relationship of identity between the disputes and prohibits the repetition of the identical: being the same the subjects and the object of the cause, the negative effect of *res judicata* is imposed, prohibiting the rediscussion of what is already defined.[19] The legal configuration of the exception of *res judicata*, it should be emphasised, presupposes not only an identity between causes, but a qualified identity, the triple identity: same parties, same claim, and same cause of action.

On the other hand, the invocation of the authority of *res judicata* assumes that *there is not* an identity between a new action and one already decided. But, as said, sometimes it is almost intuitively perceptible that, although absent the triple identity, the *res judicata* produced in a lawsuit is related to the controversy raised in another action. This is where the Lusitanian difficulties begin.

On the one hand, it is certain that the effects of *res judicata* produced in a lawsuit can only be extended to another if, between the two, there is identity. However, the

[17] João de Castro Mendes reconstructs in history the justification for such a distinction between the negative and positive effects of the adjudicated case. Specifically, in the Roman origins of the institution. See Mendes (1968), pp. 36–39.

[18] Campo DDE.

[19] Pinto (2018a), pp. 142–143.

criterion that defines such identity must be adequate to prevent the Court from being placed in a position to repeat or contradict a previous decision.[20] Otherwise, the criterion will inevitably prove to be inadequate.

Therefore, the triple identity, established by the legislator to enable the invocation of the effects of *res judicata,* is the vertex of the difficulties faced by the Portuguese doctrine to solve the cases in which, although one of its elements is not found, one perceives, nevertheless, the influence of *res judicata* on a new lawsuit.[21]

3.1.3.1 Critical Interval: How this Binomial Complicates the Visualisation of the Extent of the Objective Limits of *res judicata*. First outline on the Objective Limits of *res judicata*: Triple Identity or Decision on Material Legal Relationship?

As has been said since the beginning of this work, *res judicata* is like a coin with two sides, where the negative effects are the reverse side of the positive ones. On the negative side, it would be said that the re-discussion of the same objective controversy, involving the same facts, is prohibited. On the positive side, it can be said that, if such controversy has already been resolved by a judge in a valid process, it should be observed, even in other processes. Now, whether through the exception of *res judicata*, or through its authority, the already decided controversy cannot be repeated, but must be taken into account.[22]

Visualising *res judicata* as a single institute, with two faces, will reach the criterion of triple identity. Although it has ancient roots and is chosen by Portuguese law, triple identity is not the most appropriate criterion to establish when it is forbidden to rediscuss and it is mandatory to observe, being an improper concept to delimit the effects of *res judicata*. The hypothesis that is intended to be raised, in this topic, is

[20] This is the teleology of res judicata, as commendably, the Portuguese legislator expressly enshrined in art. 580, n. 2, of its CPC.

[21] One of the most respected portuguese proceduralists, Professor José Lebre de Freitas has already noticed the sensitivity of this point. So much so that he titled topic 2 of an important text on this topic as "An expanded concept of identity of the cause", very well noting that "to understand the triple identity of art. 581.°-1, CPC, one has to go beyond the mere verification that the second action is proposed by the same person who was one of the parties in the first against the same person who was the respective counterpart, that the request is exactly the same and that it is based (or is denied that it is based) on the same narration of constitutive facts that, in the previous action, it was intended to have integrated the forecast of the invoked legal norms." Freitas (2019), p. 694.

[22] This intuition is already in the portuguese doctrine when interpreting n. 2 of art. 580 of its CPC, visualising in this provision a prohibition of repetition and another of contradiction of the decision that has become final. See TEIXEIRA DE SOUSA. Studies on the new civil procedure, 2nd ed., 1997, p. 574, cited by Pinto (2018a), p. 147. Freitas (2019), p. 693.

that the identity between two causes that prevents the judicial pronouncement in the subsequent action is more of a *material* nature than *procedural*.[23,24]

This claim can be understood when considering the extent of the subjective effects of res judicata. That is, although the study is primarily aimed at finding the objective limits of *res judicata*, the phenomenon can be visualised in a unitary way: once the situation of the parties in relation to a certain good of life is fixed in court, the *res judicata* resulting from this fixation requires that this relationship be observed in any context, including before third parties. The legal effect of a court decision involving two subjects positioned in relation to *procedural*—plaintiff and defendant—may be relevant to a third party, as they may have an interest in discussing their right that pertains to the *substantive* relationship between those two. Thus, the relevant factor in analysing whether a dispute is resolved by the court is its position in the substantive law plane, not the procedural one.

Note that, although this statement seems to be related to the *subjective extension* of *res judicata*, this extension is only operated through its *objective delimitation.* That is, once the objective limits of what, in the court decision, is immutable and indisputable are well established, such effects are produced even before those who were not part of the process in which the *res judicata* was produced—provided it is in their favour, never to their detriment, as will be seen later.[25]

For example, in the lease of a property, there is a substantive relationship between landlord and tenant. Imagine that a third party files, against the landlord, a *rei vindicatio* action aiming to also obtain possession of the property, on the grounds of illegitimacy of the title that gives indirect possession to the defendant. Imagine that the judgement of dismissal becomes final, which expressly recognises the legitimacy of the landlord's title (of indirect possession).

---

[23] Asserting that the identity between two actions capable of making res judicata apply is "the same question of law", see Savigny (1879), pp. 258 and ss. Before that, in the same work, Savigny states that "the authority of the res judicata that belongs to the sentence is inseparable from the legal relations affirmed or denied by the judge" (p. 227). See Cabral (2012), pp. 93–97, based on Alexandre Freitas Câmara: "This second examination, constantly referred to as 'theory of identity of the legal relationship', seeks not to be tied to the formal analysis of the demand, but to seek the content of the material legal situation that is discussed in the process." João de Castro Mendes distinguishes, in the same line, the procedural and material theories of the adjudicated case. See Mendes (1968), pp. 40–42.

[24] Without giving so much confidence to this point, but already giving clues of the same path, Lebre de Freitas states that "[u]nlike the (procedural) preclusions of the right to practice the various procedural acts that precede the sentence, this preclusion manifests itself thus on the substantive law plane. The inadmissibility (...) [resulting from the prohibitions of repetition and contradiction] is nothing more than *a procedural consequence of this substantive effect:* once the legal situations of the parties are conformed by the sentence, they become indisputable" Freitas (2019), pp. 692–693, my emphasis).

[25] That is, for a party to be prevented from raising a matter to the court that decides on a legal dispute, they must have already had this opportunity once. Their procedural freedom must be respected. See below, Sect. 3.2.2.2 (Freedom in the legal regime of res judicata).

Imagine that, subsequently, the third party alleged owner turns, now, against the tenant, filing an eviction action under allegation of invalidity of the lease contract, due, again, to the illegitimacy of the landlord's indirect possession.

Note: the parties are different, the claims are different, but the *disputed substantive relationship* is the same: the real relationship regarding the legitimacy of the landlord's possession. The disputed substantive relationship in the second action was resolved (with the force of res judicata) in the first, as a preliminary issue. Such *res judicata* covers it, being forbidden to rediscuss and mandatory to observe the way the controversy was resolved, not because the triple identity was present, but because the disputed substantive relationship is the same.[26]

According to Portuguese doctrine, which strictly interprets arts. 577.°, al. "i", c/c 580.° and 581.° of its Civil Procedure Code, the tenant, now defendant in this second action, would not have an exception of *res judicata*, as they were not *party* in the process in which the *res judicata* that benefits them was formed. They could, perhaps,[27] defend themselves under the authority of the *res judicata*, as the controversy raised by the plaintiff, objectively speaking, had already been resolved.

However, what would be the point of this distinction if the [28]practical effect, in both situations, would be the same?;[29] to prohibit the rediscussion of a controversy

---

[26] As already stated and will be made explicit later, the example has an essential peculiarity for the enforceability of res judicata by a third party to be maintained, namely, that it comes to their benefit, never to their detriment—see Sect. 3.2.2.2 of this study.

[27] This uncertainty, which justifiably causes so much agony to the operators of the Portuguese legal system, could be dispelled if the restriction imposed by the concept of triple identity and the consequent distinction between the authority of res judicata and the exception of res judicata were replaced by a concept that uniformly defines the scope of the judicial pronouncement—which is the aim of this work. In this regard, Savigny states that "The identity between two actions should refer mainly to the intentio of both actions, not to the content of the judgement." Savigny (1879), p. 264.

[28] Pinto (2018a), p. 151.

[29] It is true that the dilatory exception, such as that of res judicata, prevents the court from knowing the merits of the case, as shown by art. 576, n. 2, of the Portuguese CPC (in a regime similar to that of art. 485 of the Brazilian CPC), while the authority of res judicata would involve a defence on the merits, as it would represent a fact impeding the right invoked by the plaintiff. However, it is reiterated that the practical effect is the same: the objective material controversy (in the example, the legitimacy of the landlord's possession) cannot be reconsidered, and the request based on that cause must be rejected (either because it has already been judged, or because its structures have been corroded by the prior rejection of its essential facts). Note that, in the second action (filed against the direct possessor tenant), the alleged owner could formulate his request based on other causes, in addition to the illegitimacy of the landlord's possession. If this were to happen, the dismissal of the request would not be automatic—but it would be forbidden, solely, to reconsider that specific cause, about which a decision had already been made in a previous process. The distinction between judgement on the merits or dismissal of the instance, therefore, does not help in all cases. Moreover, the artificiality of the assertion that the exception of res judicata involves dismissal of the instance becomes evident when it is observed that this exception has already been considered peremptory (with resolution on the merits) in previous legislation: art. 500, al. "a", of the CPC of 1939, art. 496, al. "a", of the CPC of 1961, up to Decree-Law no. 329-A/95, of 12 December).

already decided in court, imposing its observance. The second claim should be rejected, *regardless of whether the prohibition derives from the prohibition of rediscussing the same issue or from the imposition of observing what has already been decided about it.*

The difficulty imposed by the Portuguese legislator of only admitting the exception of *res judicata* when the triple identity is present, and only when such exception implies the resolution of the entire cause—and not when it only reaches the substantive controversy already resolved previously—has required commendable effort from the doctrine, which, not infrequently, has been expended with great methodological rigour. This difficulty reveals, however, that the real problem lies there: *res judicata* does not produce effects only when a new action triply identified with the first is at stake.[30] When the three identities are present, then the judgement should indeed be of dismissal of the instance (without resolution of the merits), precisely to avoid repetition/contradiction. But this is not the only case in which a decision that has become final influences a future claim. In fact, it is enough that the substantive controversy resolved in one action is presented again in another, either as the main object or as a preliminary issue.

In the above example, even though the triple identity is not present, the substantive controversy resolved, in both actions, is the same: the legitimacy of the landlord's possession.

Procedural modifications (both in the parties and in the claim) do not alter the legal effects that the previous judgement produced *on the substantive plane.* The substantive relationship (in this case, a real relationship) of the landlord with the property is the controversy in both procedural actions. In both cases, what the alleged owner questions is the legitimacy of one and the same substantive relationship: that which exists between the landlord and the property.

Indeed, both in the action between the landlord and the alleged owner and in the action between the latter and the tenant, the substantive controversy is one and the same: the legitimacy of the landlord's possession. Even though in the second action the landlord is not a party, but the tenant (and not as a mere substitute in the legal quality of the position), and even though the claim, in the second action, is for possession, and not for ownership, the disputed substantive relationship for the outcome is the same: the doubt about the legitimacy of the landlord's possession.[31]

[30] For an expanded perspective on the identity link between two actions capable of triggering the effects of res judicata restricted to the resolved material legal relationship, see Savigny (1879), pp. 263 ss. (For Savigny, res judicata prevents the claim that contradicts "the same legal issue" defined in a final judgement.)

[31] Another way to put this reasoning would be to say that, for the effects of res judicata to prevent the reconsideration/impose observance of an action, it would be enough to observe if the cause of the second action is resolved in the first. That is, if the essential facts alleged by the litigant, provided for in articles 5, n. 1, 552, n. 1, al. "d" and 572, al. "c" have already been resolved in a previous judgement that has become final, then the meaning given by such facts cannot be other than that given in the previous judgement. Thus, an identity of causes for the incidence of res judicata is envisaged. In this sense, res judicata does not prevent the reconsideration of an entire demand, but only of a cause. If the demand has only one cause, then, yes, the entire demand will be pre-

3.1.4 *Point, Preliminary Issue, and Incidental Decision*

Still in the phase of "clearing the field", for the purposes of this study, prejudiciality is defined as a conditioning logical link between two substantive legal relationships. There is prejudiciality when one legal relationship depends on another to some extent:[32] the solution of one. The resolution of one issue (subordinate or conditional) determines the manner in which another issue (subordinated or conditioned) should be resolved.[33]

The relationship of prejudiciality can rest on points or issues.[34] A point represents a logical link in the chain of the claim made by the plaintiff about which there is no controversy (e.g., the ownership of the vehicle in a civil damages action). On the other hand, when a link in this logical-rational chain is questioned by the

---

vented; if, however, several causes are formulated to substantiate a single request, then only the re-examination of the cause already decided in a previous process with the force of res judicata will be prevented. Therefore, for the purposes of the incidence of res judicata (both positive and negative) there is no need for identity of parties, requests and cause, this last repetition being sufficient: the essential thing is that the essential facts in question are identical, because such facts always relate to material legal relationships, not procedural ones.

[32] Exposing the substantive doctrine of the relationship of prejudiciality of Enrico Allorio adopted here, and closely following the lessons of Francesco Menestrina, see, among all, Moreira (1967), passim, especially pp. 38 and ss. This, the "nesso di dipendenza sostanziale", also seems to be the doctrine upheld by Pisani (2021), p. 328.

[33] The definition of prejudiciality can be further refined, classifying it, as the doctrine usually does, into logical or legal—as done by Moreira (1967), pp. 43–54, or into logical or technical—as proposed by Pisani (2021), pp. 326–329.

[34] Although the establishment of a dispute over a "point", transforming it into an "issue", represents a dispensable element for the relationship of prejudiciality, as such a relationship may relate to a legal effect that the judge is authorised to resolve ex officio, it represents an essential element for the purpose of defining the extent of the effects of res judicata, since it supposedly incorporates respect for the dictates of due process, as will be demonstrated later, in Sect. 3.2.2.2.

defendant, casting doubt on a point through which the judicial reasoning must necessarily pass to decide the claim, the point becomes an *issue*.[35,36]

As this study focuses on the extent of the effects of *res judicata*, the relevant prejudiciality here is that which is related to points in the logical chain of the claim that have been disputed by the parties, or on which there is legal uncertainty—that is, on an *issue*.[37]

Thus, a prejudicial issue can be defined as a doubt about a legal effect asserted or refuted by one of the parties that logically precedes the claim, conditioning it in some way, and which is the subject of controversy in the process.[38]

---

[35] Article 282 of the Brazilian CPC of 1939 established the possibility of the judge concentrating, in the judgement, the decisions regarding preliminary issues and the merits of the case, except when there was incompatibility between them, which reveals the insufficiency of the topographic criterion to understand the meaning of a preliminary issue and also indicates the insufficiency of traditional topographic criteria (judgement, request, etc.) for identifying the objective limits of res judicata, as will be attempted to demonstrate later. See, below, Sect. 4.2 (Topology of res judicata from the perspective of the judgement: in the device or in the reasoning?). In addition, the same old Brazilian CPC provided, in the sole paragraph of its article 287, that "issues that constitute a necessary premise for conclusion" would be considered decided, implying that, although the word "issue" was used, it would refer to mere logical antecedents, disputed or not, legitimising Alfredo Buzaid's theory of "implicit judgements" (From the appeal of petition, 2nd ed., 1956, p. 113, cited in Silva (1979), pp. 119–121, rejected in this study. In the same vein, Ovídio Baptista da Silva himself, considering irrelevant the "actual dispute" about the claim formulated exclusively in the initial, stating that "the issues implicitly contained in this dispute must be covered, inexorably, by res judicata, if they constitute a logical antecedent necessary for the express solution of the final decision." (p. 122). Cf Alvim et al. (2016), p. 615.

[36] The presentation is simplified, as stated, as a measure to seek conciseness, clarity and objectivity, as much as to avoid verbosity. For an extended understanding of the elements of the logical-procedural chain that, in different ways, can manifest prejudiciality in a procedural relationship (meticulously working the concepts of point, doubtful point, controversial point, prejudicial point, issue, main issue, preliminary issue, preliminary issue, prejudicial issue, incidental issue, cause and prejudicial cause) and the types of prejudicial issues (in a broad/strict sense, proper/improper, remote/near, mediate/immediate, total/partial, to the action/to the judgement, internal/internal, homogeneous/heterogeneous, mandatory/optional), cf. Cavalcanti (2019), pp. 158–178.

[37] In fact, on a point, issue or cause. But the latter is not relevant for the present study, referring more to the need for suspension of the process to await the solution of a prejudicial cause discussed in another simultaneous process. Cf. Moreira (1967), pp. 48–49, supported by the doctrine of Francesco Menestrina, Alberto Romano and Francesco Carnelutti. Cf. also, Pisani (2021), p. 329. For Castro Mendes, "an issue is therefore the alternative posed by two assertions, only one of which is necessarily true." Mendes (1963), p. 297, footnote n. 1. In another work, the great portuguese professor defines a prejudicial issue, including, in the definition adopted here, the need for the dispute that forms the prejudicial issue to be the subject of an autonomous action—an apparently unjustifiable restriction. Cf. Mendes (1968), p. 196.

[38] This definition encompasses the two species of prejudiciality—logical and technical—identified by Proto Pisani. For him, technical prejudiciality is the one that reveals the dependence of one legal relationship on another. That is, for a legal relationship to exist, it is necessary to recognise the existence of another legal relationship, such as the relationship of kinship/paternity is necessary for the relationship of alimentary credit. One can speak of a "conditioning legal relationship" and a "conditioned legal relationship". The relationship of technical prejudiciality is a relationship of absolute subordination, or existence, and not merely relative, or mode. Logical prejudiciality is the

For example, paternity in a maintenance action, fault in tort liability, the validity of the contract in the pursuit of contractual performance, ownership in compensation for the loss of the property, the legitimacy of the landlord's indirect possession in an eviction action brought against the tenant.

If the conditioning point is disputed in the process—that is, if there is a prejudicial issue—for the judge to be able to decide on the maintenance claim, it is essential that he decides, first, on paternity. To decide on the compensation claim based on subjective civil liability, the judge needs to decide, first, on the offender's fault. To decide on the obligation to fulfil a contractual duty, it is necessary to consider the validity of the contract. And so on.

If the point is not disputed, then it is assumed to resolve the claim. And the lack of controversy about it dispenses with an express decision. The lack of decision, in turn, leads to the impossibility of extending the effects of *res judicata*.

The prejudicial issue, therefore, represents an *issue* whose controversy *prejudices* the analysis of the claim and, therefore, needs to be *decided*. This decision is called *incidental*, because its object is not the main process. An incidental decision, in these terms, is, therefore, one that does not fall on the main object of the demand, but on its antecedent/conditioning. Nevertheless, it is still a decision on an issue about which the parties have disputed, as it concerns legal effects arising from facts alleged by one party and refuted by another.

It would be different if a link in the logical chain leading to the acceptance of the claim is not the subject of procedural controversy. Although such a link may be a prerequisite for the decision, it is not, properly, a decision. For example, the plaintiff, allegedly a son, claims maintenance against an uncontroversial father. In this case, although paternity is assumed at the time of the judgement of the claim, there is no *decision* regarding this prejudicial relationship underlying it.

The hypothesis here supported, that the effects of *res judicata* are extendable to the decision on prejudicial issues, therefore, presupposes that the *prejudicial point* is disputed, and therefore, that there is an express decision about it (and, consequently, that, before it, all the procedural guarantees that conform to due process of law have been assured to the parties). That is why it has been said here that *res judicata* extends to the decision on a *prejudicial issue* (and not to "grounds"), provided certain requirements are observed. In truth, as is evident, what induces *res judicata* is the *decision* pronounced on the prejudicial issue.

---

one that connects different demands in a complex legal relationship—like the complex borrower relationship in relation to the request for condemnation to the payment of a late instalment. The subordinating particle is constitutive, impeding, modifying or extinguishing the subordinate relationship. According to Pisani, the majority Italian jurisprudence has established that "the objective limits of res judicata always extend to the entire complex legal relationship constituting the single legal effect immediately brought to trial as petitum, with the consequence that, for example, the condemnation to payment of the rent also makes a statement regarding the previous existence and validity of the entire lease relationship or the judgement, passed in res judicata, of condemnation to payment of a single instalment of the mortgage makes a statement regarding the existence and validity of the mortgage in its entirety." Pisani (2021), p. 327.

3.2 Values, Legal Principles, and Functions of *Res Judicata*

The intensification and longevity of the dispute about the extent of the objective effects of *res judicata* make one disbelieve in a single and definitive answer. However, the academic task requires that one does not give up seeking it. There are, at least, more or less sustainable positions. The support of the positions, however, will always rest on something more solid than it. The argument is supported both by its rationality and by the strength of the value on which it rests.

It cannot be taken for granted that all of society regulated by a set of legal norms agrees on the degree of stability it considers most appropriate for a judicial decision. On the other hand, it cannot be denied that the justification for this optimal stabilising degree is based on a certain value or on how it interacts with others. Applying this premise to the object under study, it can be said that the justification for *res judicata* having a certain reach necessarily rests on the valuation of a certain good or on the relationship between goods intertwined in *res judicata*.[39]

In a multipolarised, pluralistic, and relativistic society, where ethical consensuses are scarce (perhaps extinct), scientific knowledge cannot be produced without revealing the axiological premises that underlie it. The scientificity of knowledge in the argumentative area, such as the Science of Law, derives from the possibility of guiding it back to a core that can be referred to as "common", intersubjectively connectable—even so that it can be criticised and, eventually, revised.

Therefore, to support the hypothesis that decisions on prejudicial issues should be stabilised by res judicata, as well as to impose conditions for such stability to occur, it is necessary to ask what values interact at the heart of this hypothesis. And more than that, for certain values to impact legal institutions such as *res judicata*, it is necessary to ask what are the legal principles that incorporate such values into the legal system. The legal protection of values through norms of the principle type (and

[39] Despite being fascinating, the theme of values is also one of the most tangled. Thus, it is not intended here to delve into it. However, for the purpose of continuing the reasoning, value is defined as the measure of the good. This concept will be illustrated with an image familiar to legal professionals: the scales. Value is the weight placed on one side of the scales to measure the goodness of the object placed on the other side. The extent to which a particular phenomenon is considered good, that is the value assigned to that phenomenon. Every good generates a value. Those goods that are better than others are more highly valued. From a legal perspective, a low value results in legal indifference. A high value leads to its legalisation, in proportion. The lack of significant value of a good makes it dispensable from a legal perspective and, therefore, it does not become part of the legal system through a codified norm. The absence of a norm regarding a particular good is a manifestation of the insignificance of its value to that society. Conversely, the substantial legal regulation of a good reveals its high valuation by that society. For example: the complex network of norms that regulate taxation as a means to carry out state activities on one hand; the legal indifference regarding the amount of insecticide used to exterminate insects in a residence on the other. The more value a good has for a particular society, the more it relies on the law to protect it, legalising it through codified rules or principles. Thus, a sequence is envisaged: good → value → norm (rule or principle).

also by those of the rule type) is identified with the functions of legal institutions.[40] What is the purpose of *res judicata*? What function (or functions) does it perform in the system? How do the values embedded in this institution relate and how do the principles (and rules) that shape them impose themselves on each other?

Having completed the first part of this work, in which the main concepts related to the problem developed here were outlined and, possibly, criticised, we now proceed to discuss the values and legal principles that, in the author's view, underpin the controversy, paving a path that seeks to balance the position defended here.

3.2.1 Bauman and the Golden Formula: Security and Freedom in a Love–Hate Relationship

Zygmunt Bauman presents a fascinating reading of Freud's *Civilisation and Its Discontents*. For Bauman,

> there are two essential values that are absolutely indispensable for a satisfying, rewarding and relatively happy life: security and freedom. There is no dignity in the absence of one of them. Security without freedom is slavery; freedom without security is chaos, the impossibility of doing, planning or even dreaming about anything. We need both. The problem is that so far, no one has found the golden formula, the perfect mix of security and freedom. Every time you gain a bit of security, you give up a bit of freedom; every time you gain more freedom, you give up some measure of security.[41]

[40] As shown by the prestigious Theory of Principles by Humberto Ávila, which connects the concept of a legal principle with an ideal state of affairs to be pursued—therefore, with a function to be performed. Cf. Ávila (2022), Here too there is a deep connection with the so-called Aristotelian "theory of virtues", which includes a conception of teleological justice. That is, the criterion of justice derives from the ends of a particular good. The value of something is related to the performance of its function Cf. Aristotle (2020).

[41] Interview given by Bauman to Fernando Schüller and Mário Mazzilli, team of Fronteiras do Pensamento, on 25 July 2011, at his residence in Leeds (London), accessible at https://www.fronteiras.com/leia/exibir/zygmunt-bauman-liberdade-e-seguranca-um-caso-de-amor-e-odio and on the Fronteiras do Pensamento YouTube Channel (https://www.youtube.com/@fronteiras), specifically at https://www.youtube.com/watch?v=POZcBNo-D4A, at 22min30s. Supplement at https://www.fronteiras.com/assista/exibir/seguranca-e-liberdade-uma-dicotomia. In all cases, accessed on 08/08/2025. According to Bauman, Freud saw civilisation as an exchange: something of value is given to receive something of value. For Freud, the generation at the beginning of the last century had given up too much freedom in favour of security, leading to an excessively rigid, "castrating" society. Many "no's", many renunciations. Bauman suggests that all this hermeticism produced a reaction. It's like Newton's third law applied to society: for every action there is a reaction of the same proportion and in the opposite direction. Excess security demands an increase in freedom. A century after Freud's observation, Bauman believes that we have given up too much security in exchange for freedom. We live in an insecure society, without form, without structure (hence the "post-structuralists"). However, where there is an excess of freedom, security will end up regaining lost ground... From this swinging pendulum of history was born an interesting collection of essays analysed by a psychoanalyst called The Return of the Pendulum, in which Bauman discusses the historical-social oscillation between security and freedom, as this excerpt reveals: "That is why civilisation is a business, insists Freud: to get something from it, human beings have

This is the dilemma of the extent of the effects of *res judicata*: How much security must be given up to obtain the necessary freedom? How much freedom must be surrendered to have the essential security for a dignified life? As the brilliant Polish sociologist predicted, no one has yet found the "golden formula" that perfectly balances the two,[42] and it is not the intention to do so in this modest study. However,

to give up something else. Both the goods obtained and those given up in exchange are valued and fervently desired; therefore, each successive exchange formula is nothing more than a temporary arrangement, the product of a transaction never fully satisfactory to either party of this flameless, perpetual antagonism. The discord would subside if it were possible to attend to individual desires and social demands at the same time. But this will not happen. To achieve a satisfactory life - or bearable, livable, to be more precise - freedoms to act according to one's own impulses, urgencies, inclinations and desires are as indispensable as the restrictions imposed in the interest of security, since security without freedom would equate to slavery, while freedom without security would unleash chaos, disorientation and perpetual uncertainty, resulting in an inability to act decisively. But both are and will forever be irreconcilable." Bauman (2017), p. 16.

[42]The soudness of Bauman's argument, contrasting security and freedom as fundamental and mutually alterophagic values, is confirmed not only by its Freudian origin but also by its identification, more than thirty years earlier, by another thinker, from a very different tradition from the two. The celebrated North American reformed sociologist Francis Schaeffer, analysing the central sociological argument of the 60th anniversary special edition of Time magazine titled The most amazing 60 years in history, stated: "*In this essay Time has given that which indeed is central, namely the problem of form and freedom. It is a problem which every culture from the beginning of history has had to confront. The problem is this: If there is not a proper* ***balance between form and freedom****, then the society will move into either of two extremes. Freedom, without a proper balance of form, will lead to chaos and to the total breakdown of society. Form, without a proper balance of freedom, will lead to authoritarianism, and to the destruction of individual and social freedom. But note further: no society can exist in a state of chaos. And whenever chaos has reigned for even a short time, it has given birth to the imposition of arbitrary control.*" Schaeffer (1984), p. 18, my emphasis. Aside from the subtle difference in names (security and freedom for Bauman, form and freedom for Schaeffer), the similarity between the texts is striking. While Freud argued that the "discontent of his civilisation" in the 1920s was that that generation had surrendered too much freedom in favour of security, producing a rigid, hermetic, "castrating" society (in psychoanalytic language), Schaeffer would anticipate Bauman's announcement about the pendulum swing of history. Excessive "no's", excessive renunciations, would trigger a reaction movement, like Newton's Third Law applied to society: "yes's" (pardon the pun for the English language) for everything and everyone—"let's allow ourselves", as Lulu Santos would say in Modern Times. Excess security demands increased freedom. A hundred years later, we can see the result of the reaction (of equal force and in the opposite direction, as Newton taught): in postmodernity, perhaps we can say that we have surrendered too much security in exchange for freedom. We live in an insecure society, without form, without structure (hence the "post-structuralists", like Foucault, Derrida and Nietzsche himself, in the moral plane). Everyone does what they want, not what is good. In fact, there is no longer a "good", a "right", a "virtue". What there is, is a will to power (connecting Nietzsche to Freud). But the pendulum of history is inexorable: where there is excess freedom, security will regain lost ground. The authoritarian and liberal governments that have been alternating over the last 100 years around the globe confirm the thesis. For a deeper understanding of Schaeffer's view on form and freedom, cf. the Inaugural Lecture of the L'Abri Brazil School of Theology and Christian Life of 2022, delivered by Guilherme de Carvalho, available at https://www.youtube.com/watch?v=v1V_SAci6M8&t=2338s, on the channel https://www.youtube.com/@labribrasil, accessed on 08/08/2025.

there is a gain in recognising, in terms of awareness, that the choice comes not only with benefits but also with losses.

One can choose to privilege the "freedom" to discuss, to keep issues open, to have them available and potentially favourable or subject to improvement: flexibility. One may prefer to restrict the effects of *res judicata* to the minimum necessary to produce only that fundamental security, leaving as many controversies as possible so that they can be settled with the greatest possible precision.

Or one can choose to privilege the "security" of knowing what to count on, what one is dealing with, the certainty and clarity about what is and what is not, what can and cannot be: stability. One may prefer to extend the effects of *res judicata* as much as possible to produce all the security that can be produced, dissolving all the controversies that fit into the discussion minimally already carried out in the judicial process.

By opting for one, one is prioritising a value of extreme relevance. However, the enhancement of this value occurs at the expense, and in the exact proportion, according to Bauman, of another value of identical fundamentality.

Defining the extent of the effects of *res judicata* involves a choice:

(a) greater contestability/revisability: Should every controversy involving any person always be subject to judicial verification? Should the distribution of justice be as precise/exact as possible, advocating for a more detailed, meticulous, specific *res judicata*? Or:
(b) greater indisputability/stability: Should the disputability of controversies be restricted to the minimum necessary? Should the distribution of justice be as pacifying and universalising as possible, advocating for ensuring that controversies are resolved in an amplified manner?

To be didactic: imagine that legal uncertainty is a patient with multiple complaints, suffering from several different pathologies. One can cure him with the use of various specific treatments for each disease, in a slow and costly manner, but without side effects. Or one can cure him by administering a single generalist treatment, which combats all diseases, but with many side effects. The former would be the more restricted *res judicata*; the latter, more extensive.

The extent of the effects of *res judicata* is tied to the State's heteronomous imposition on individuals' freedom. The greater its extent, the more the force of the State is felt in fulfilling its primary mission: to ensure social peace. The lesser extent of *res judicata*, on the other hand, represents greater freedom of individuals in relation to the State. But also, less freedom of the individual in relation to himself or, from a certain perspective, in relation to other individuals. Bauman's golden formula between security and freedom is exactly the relentless pursuit of the ideal size of the State. As aptly noted by Francis Schaeffer, an excess of security leads to authoritarianism; a lack of it, however, leads to chaos.[43] Neither of these extremes is desirable and the perfect balance between the two is utopian. Therefore, it is necessary to

[43] See citation from the footnote above.

argue around the choice of the resting point on this spectrum between security and freedom so that, at least regarding the limits of *res judicata*, a reasonable solution can be reached.

In establishing the extent of *res judicata*, security and freedom play important roles for the Rule of Law: respectively, broad pacification of disputes and broad disputability of disputes. In weighing the two, two risks present themselves: subjecting the parties to the indisputability of unjust decisions or to the disputability of fair decisions.[44] If one opts to give greater weight to freedom, one will prefer not to have certainty about legal relations than to have a sub-optimal resolution. If greater weight is given to security, one will prefer a sub-optimal decision to not having legal certainty.

Another value, besides security and freedom, more restricted than them and of a more instrumental character, which can influence the definition of the limits of *res judicata*, is that of the instrumentality of the process. Procedural law entangles itself in the rigour of technical concepts such as dispute, request, cause of action, principle of concentration, principle of demand, efficacy/force/quality/effects, etc. In the scientific endeavour to maintain the rigour and purity of the definitions that give these concepts, they relegate to the background the performance of the ultimate mission of the process, namely, to enable the State-Judge to realise the substantive law invoked by the parties. What is wanted, with the process, is to provide the best and swiftest jurisdiction.[45]

---

[44] By fair and unfair decisions, we are not referring to the merit of the decision, but rather to the procedure that leads to it according to Luhmann (1980), pp. 48–113. Specifically, as is obvious, we are talking about the delimitation of the portion, within what has been decided, that becomes indisputable. That is, we are talking about the extent of the effects of res judicata.

[45] Carlos Alberto Alvaro de Oliveira dedicated his academic life to unfolding the values of security and effectiveness, balancing them within his value-formalism as a set of values that serve an end: to ensure the material justice of the decision. For the late proceduralist from Rio Grande do Sul, "it is necessary to rethink the problem [of the balance of values that underpin the process] as a whole, to verify the political, cultural and axiological aspects of the conditioning and determining factors of the structuring and organisation of the process, to finally establish the foundations of value-formalism. And this is because its ordering, organising and coordinating power is not hollow, empty or blind, for there is no formalism for formalism's sake. It is only permissible to think about the concept insofar as it serves to organise a fair process and serves to achieve the ultimate purposes of the process in a reasonable time and, above all, to contribute to the material justice of the decision. When meditating on the external factors of formalism, thought immediately tends, in a very broad initial schematic formulation, to focus on the ends of the process, and the notion of end is necessarily intertwined with the value or values to be ideally achieved through the process. Therefore, an analysis of the most important values for the process is imposed: on the one hand, the achievement of material justice and social peace, on the other, effectiveness, security and fair internal organisation of the process itself (fair trial). (...) Effectiveness and security present themselves as essential values for shaping the process in this or that direction, with a view to satisfying certain purposes, also serving to guide the judge in the application of rules and principles." Oliveira (2017), p. 65. The thesis: Oliveira, 1996. Later transformed into a book: Oliveira (2010). João de Castro Mendes places other dishes on the balance of res judicata. Instead of security and freedom, the Portuguese professor senses that the extent of the effects of res judicata is balanced between justice and security. Cf. Mendes (1968), p. 120.

This brief reflection, developed with the intention of provoking the weighing of two values that collide in the controversy about the extent of *res judicata*, should be guided by the teleology of the process, namely, justice, whether materialised in stability or in flexibility. In any case, emphasising the instrumental character of the process before the substantive law, the balance between freedom and security in defining the limits of *res judicata* should be guided by the search for the best realisation of substantive law. Instead of clinging to the theoretical concepts involved in *res judicata*, one should, without losing scientific rigour, ask the following question: *How* should the State provide jurisdiction—providing more security or providing more freedom? Or, what is even superior: How to balance to the maximum extent both—security and freedom—so that jurisdiction is provided in the fairest possible way?

3.2.2 *More Security or More Freedom?*

Security and freedom are values unquestionably incorporated into various legal systems through the positivisation of numerous rules and principles.

Regarding the extent of the effects of *res judicata*, the value of security is fundamentally linked to its homonymous principle, legal certainty. It is also linked to procedural economy and the efficiency of judicial administration.

On the other hand, the value of freedom infiltrates the legal system, from the perspective of the extent of the effects of *res judicata*, through the principle of *procedural due process of law*, especially through its sub-principles, namely the inalienability of jurisdiction, the principle of demand, the adversarial principle, and the principle of full defence.

3.2.2.1 Security in the Legal Framework of *Res Judicata*

3.2.2.1.1 Legal Certainty

There is no intention here to delve into the vast principle of legal certainty. Brief considerations about it will be limited to what is strictly relevant to apply it to the problem of the extent of the effects of *res judicata*.[46]

As repeatedly stated, the most evident effect of *res judicata* is a coin with two faces: on one side, the prohibition of re-discussion about what is decided, the prohibitive face; on the other, the need to observe what is decided, the imperative face. Indeed, *res judicata* stabilises the content of a judicial decision, making it, as widely

[46] For further considerations on legal security, see, among many others, Ávila (2021).

admitted in Brazilian procedural law (and in art. 502 of the Brazilian CPC), "immutable and indisputable".[47]

The immutability and indisputability of the content of the judicial decision basically provide two benefits to the parties and those who engage in legal relations with them: certainty and stability.

There are simple and concordant legal relations, unfolding with a strong fraternal bond. In this case, there are not many disputes or doubts. But there are also complex and antagonised relations, primarily individualised. The parties occupying poles in this latter type of relation can often find themselves uncertain about the legal effects that result from the acts they perform or performed by the counterparty in this relation. This uncertainty halts, so to speak, the relation. The trade of legal goods is obstructed. And, as astutely observed by Bauman, "[l]iving under conditions of prolonged or seemingly incurable uncertainty entails two equally humiliating sensations: that of ignorance (not knowing what one will face in the future) and that of impotence (being unable to influence one's own course)".[48]

According to the teaching of Castro Mendes, "being the conduct of man as a rational being, directed by his knowledge, that is, by the affirmations he chose to take as the basis of his action, this implies as a normal task of man the *resolution of situations of uncertainty*".[49] And, further on, it continues by stating that "[t]o the legal order, notably through the institution of *civil proceedings*, it is more interested in preparing for the future than in reconstructing the past".[50]

The conflict inherent in such a relationship shakes the entire community, being contrary to social peace and, therefore, to the objectives of the Rule of Law[51] that is so committed to building a free, fair, and solidary society.[52]

Understanding how the State, holder of the monopoly of coercive imposition of legal force, comprehends such a formerly obtuse relationship, gives the parties autonomy. That is, it allows them to know, in advance, the consequences of their actions, and therefore, allows them to act with greater agility and freedom.[53] The

---

[47] And perhaps one could add: binding. The portuguese expression inscribed in art. 619, n. 1, of the CPC, is very apt: "binding force".

[48] Bauman (2017), p. 17. And the author continues: "And there is no doubt that both [ignorance and impotence] are demeaning: in our highly individualised society, in which it is presumed (against the evidence of the facts, so to speak) that each individual must bear full responsibility for his or her life's destiny, these sensations suggest the incompetence of the person concerned to tackle the tasks that other people, apparently more successful, seem to carry out thanks to greater skill and better effort".

[49] Mendes (1968), p. 11.

[50] Mendes (1968), p. 15.

[51] "With res judicata, (...) in a pragmatic way, certainty and security of the Law are guaranteed, an indispensable condition for life in society." Varela et al. (1985), p. 705.

[52] Objective of the Federative Republic of Brazil (art. 3, I, of the CRFB) fundamental principle of the Portuguese Republic (art. 1 of the CRP).

[53] We must not lose sight of the curious paradox here: in the clash between security and freedom, it is concluded that security produces freedom.

certainty about certain legal acts of the relationship makes it more fluid. The parties become more confident. The trade of legal goods becomes more unimpeded.

Moreover, where there is uncertainty, there is no projection of the future. Without trust (*trustfulness*) there is no rest (*reliability*), the relationship does not progress, it does not develop. It stalls.

And, once you know what to count on, there must be stability to produce confidence. It is necessary not only to know what to count on but also to know that what is known will remain as it is, at least as long as it is reasonable to expect that it will remain so. Minimum longevity.

Thus, certainty and stability generate anticipation, planning, cognisability, predictability, autonomy, continuity, deepening, trust, intensified circulation. All these benefits are added to a legal relationship that has its controversial points defined with immutability and indisputability, with the force of *res judicata*, therefore.

3.2.2.1.2 Coherence

Coherence is the attribute that allows grouping distinct particles under a common criterion. It is a trait of rationality in the system.[54] Rationality opposes arbitrariness—and, therefore, also integrates the model of the *Rule of Law* (instead of the *Rule of Men*). In a rational world, things cannot be and not be at the same time. The paradox generates perplexity. And perplexity paralyses. The inconsistency of being at one moment and not-being at another generates insecurity. Insecurity, in turn, generates loss of autonomy. What is not defined can turn into a loss, and a loss of unknown magnitude. And perhaps this implies that the insecure subject decides not to advance, not to conduct his life over such indefiniteness, fearful of the unknown consequences. Therefore, legal relationships are stalled and the transit of legal goods embedded in these relationships are retained.

The extension of the objective effects of *res judicata* to decisions on prejudicial issues protects such issues against incoherence, as it makes them immutable and indisputable. Whenever they are called to compose a decision, they will be defined in a binding manner. Whenever they are part of a relationship, it will be known what is being dealt with.

3.2.2.1.3 Judicial Authority, Procedural Economy, and Judicial Efficiency

Ensuring that certain controversies already assessed and decided by a judge are put beyond question reinforces judicial authority. The Rule of Law is one in which the Law prevails, and is not at the mercy of the parties, available for them, at their discretion, to manipulate it in a way to make it subservient. The rule is that of the Law, and not that of arbitrariness or the convenience of men.

---

[54] Baini (2011), p. 106.

The rejection of inconsistent decisions is at the base of the concern with the efficiency of the performance of the activity of distributing jurisdiction.[55] For the Rule of Law to be effective—in other words, for the State to be a Rule of Law— judicial decisions, as emanations of the materialisation of the Law, must produce effects to their maximum extent. This is also legal security, under the aspect of effectiveness.

Thus, extending the effects of *res judicata* to decisions on prejudicial issues increases the credibility of the judicial institution, which radiates effects beyond the parties to the process, as it generates a general feeling of trust in public institutions. But it radiates effects, mainly, to the subjects with whom the parties to the process in which the *res judicata* was produced will relate.

In addition, the extension of the effects of *res judicata* to prejudicial issues represents economy. Procedural economy, as it enhances the jurisdictional function in order to secure the legal content of more than one controversy with a single procedural act, giving it maximum efficiency. And also financial economy—both for the parties and for the society that, collectively, supports the judicial apparatus.

In this regard, art. 580, n. 2, of the Portuguese CPC, deserves reference. The purpose of res judicata is "to avoid that the court is placed in the alternative of contradicting or reproducing a previous decision". Contradicting a previous decision would be a problem of coherence, it would generate instability, uncertainty. And reproducing a previous decision would simply be a waste—of time, of effort, and of money.

3.2.2.2 Freedom in the Legal Framework of *Res Judicata*

On the one hand, there are many reasons to tip the balance of the extension of the effects of *res judicata* towards security, there are just as many reasons why one could argue that *res judicata* should be restricted as much as possible.

The way the argument of this chapter is organised—starting with the presentation of the reasons that reveal the importance of security and then moving on to the reasons that reinforce the need for freedom—is not casual. The previous paragraph also reveals this: the greater or lesser extent of the effects of *res judicata* is more a question of more or less security than of freedom. And the reason is quite evident: *res judicata* serves security. The question is to know *how much* security is wanted. Or, put another way, how much freedom is given up to have security? Or, still, how much freedom is wanted to inject into the security promoted by *res judicata*? How much freedom is necessary for the security promoted by *res judicata* to be balanced?

The grains of salt with which freedom, so to speak, seasons the recipe of the extension of the effects of *res judicata* are fundamental to test the hypothesis here sustained: if it is true that *res judicata* can produce effects on decisions about prejudicial issues (and, therefore, for more security to be produced), what are the

[55] Verstal, Allan. Res judicata: Preclusion. New York: Mathew Bender, 1969. pp. 7, 10 and 12, cited by Marinoni (2018), p. 49.

conditions for this to occur (i.e., how much freedom should be preserved in this incursion of security on the terrain of the extension of the effects of *res judicata*)?

As already announced, the legal principle that coats the grains of salt of freedom that interfere in the recipe of the optimal extension of the effects of *res judicata* is the *procedural due process of law*, especially in derived subprinciples, that of the inalienability of jurisdiction, of the device, of the demand, of the contradictory, and of the ample defence.

3.2.2.2.1 Procedural Due Process of Law

Just like legal security, the *procedural due process of law*[56] is one of those legal principles whose exploration demands extra stamina. It is not, therefore, an intention to exhaust it, nor to deepen it. The little that will be explored about it is limited to be essential for the understanding of the argument of this study.[57]

One of the greatest legal documents in history is the mythical *Magna Carta*, of King John I, the Landless. One of the elements that makes it so great is, without a doubt, the clause of the *due process*.[58] According to this clause, reproduced, in essence, in the 5th Amendment to the Constitution of the United States of America and also in (quoted literally below, for its simplicity) art. 5°, LIV, of the CRFB, "no one shall be deprived of liberty or property without due process of law".[59]

It is, therefore, exactly as in the context of the *Magna Chata*, *mutatis mutandis,* one of the main manifestations of freedom in the legal sphere: to restrict the state power to interfere in the freedom of individuals, requiring that such intervention always be preceded by a formal process.[60]

---

[56] The anglophone terminology of the principle was chosen to avoid the ambiguity generated by its bifurcation, in the vernacular, between the brazilian ("due legal process") and portuguese ("equitable process") constitutional systems, respectively provided for in art. 5, LIV, of the CRFB and art. 20, n. 4, of the CRP. The principle was also used with its specified nomenclature, adjectivising the due process with its forename procedural, in order to distinguish it and avoid confusion with its co-brother developed by the US Supreme Court, the substantive due process of law.

[57] For a deeper understanding of the procedural due process of law, one can see, among many, Vitorelli (2018). Also, see: Mariotti (2008), Wasserman (2004) and Mattos (2009).

[58] In the abbreviated reissue of the Magna Charta made in 1354, clause n. 29 had the following wording: "No man of what state or condition he be, shall be put out of his lands or tenements nor taken, nor disinherited, nor put to death, without he be brought to answer by due process of law". Clause n. 39 of the original expanded wording (year 1215) had identical content, but without the expression "due process of law". Cf. Vitorelli (2018), p. 189.

[59] The Portuguese Constitution has a similar content rule, although less explicit, in n. 4 and 5 of art. 20. Other Constitutions also enshrine it with some formula: Italy, arts. 24 and 111; Spain, art. 24; Germany, art. 103. The due process has a formula also enshrined at the international level in the Universal Declaration of Human Rights (1948, arts. 8 and 10), in the European Convention on Human Rights (1950, art. 6), in the International Covenant on Civil and Political Rights (1966, art. 14) and in the American Convention on Human Rights (1969, art. 8).

[60] It is interesting to note that Paul of Tarsus, around the year 50 AD (therefore, more than a thousand years before the Magna Charta) used the prerogative of a Roman citizen to demand clarifica-

In addition, the *due process* imposes that the intervention in individual freedom only occurs following a certain procedure, which is permeated by a set of values that ensure the legitimacy of this intervention. Some of these values directly linked to the controversy about the extension of the effects of *res judicata* will be succinctly indicated below.

3.2.2.2.2 Ingredients of a Procedural Recipe for Freedom in *Res Judicata*: Action, Inalienability of Jurisdiction, Device, Demand, Congruence, Contradiction, and Ample Defence

The state power to establish *res judicata* is limited, ultimately, by the parties' will to submit to this power. For it is up to the parties to elect the matter about which they postulate jurisdiction. From this, it follows that the judge cannot sentence beyond what has been asked of him. The principle of the device (the parties dispose of what they want to ask and allege) connects to that of the demand (the procedural content discussed, the object of the dispute, is defined by the parties, both in the request and in the defence). And this to the congruence between request and sentence.[61] The power to imprint legal force coercively cannot be entirely available to the judge for him to voluntarily move the state apparatus—the Leviathan! —against an individual. After all, this would be exactly the opposite of the *due process*. Such power needs to be limited, and it is through the will of the parties, who put in the hands of the judge the limits, of what they deliberate to risk. They are the parties, therefore, who establish the limits of jurisdictional action.

Therefore, the State cannot decide on something about which it has not been provoked. But, more than that, the State cannot decide on something about which it has not given the parties the opportunity to sustain their reasons and produce their evidence. The right to be heard before having a decision against him, as well as the right to influence the judge's conviction by presenting reasons—the so-called formal and material contradiction—and, also, the right to present evidence of his allegations—the so-called ample defence—are part of the most rigid core of the *due process*.

Moreover, imposing on someone to submit to jurisdictional command without the possibility of discussing the content of this command offends the most fundamental procedural right enshrined in any civilised legal system: the right to action itself and the principle of the inalienability of jurisdiction, according to which no injury or threat of injury can be excluded from the Judiciary's consideration.[62]

---

tion from his tormentors, denoting the presence of this value as an ingredient of freedom over public-state interventions already in Ancient Rome: "Being Roman citizens, they publicly flogged us without formal process and threw us into prison. And now they want to get rid of us secretly? No! Let them come themselves and free us". Acts of the Apostles, 16.37 (NIV).

[61] Art. 5, n. 1, in conjunction with art. 609, n. 1, of the Portuguese CPC; art. 492 of the Brazilian CPC.

[62] Art. 5, XXXV, CRFB.

A judicial decision with the force of *res judicata* affecting an individual who did not have an adequate opportunity to influence that decision characterises an abusive state interference with freedom. Such a decision, in truth, represents arbitrariness and violates the democratic principle, as in the contemporary constitutional state each citizen (and not just those who had access to *due process* and obtained a favourable decision) must be treated with equal consideration and respect.

A composition of these three sub-principles—of demand, of contradiction, and of ample defence— leads to the parties, when in court, needing to know what is at stake in order to decide how they will behave, what degree of investment they will make to influence the judgement. The parties dedicate themselves to the resolution of the dispute in exact proportion to the interference of that decision on their life and their assets, deciding what they will allege (and, therefore, to what extent they will allow State interference in their freedom) and how much effort they intend to expend to prove their allegations.

Indeed, for decisions on prejudicial issues to produce the effect of *res judicata*, it is necessary that the principles of demand, contradiction, and ample defence are observed. This means that a decision on an incidental issue cannot produce *res judicata* if the parties have not invoked jurisdiction, have not had the opportunity to influence the court's conviction, have not had their arguments taken into account, or have not had the opportunity to present evidence of their allegations.

3.2.3 *The Golden Formula: Security and Freedom Balanced in* Res Judicata

These are the requirements for the objective effects of *res judicata* to reach the decision made on a prejudicial issue to the main claim. Every prejudicial issue, to be resolved with the force of *res judicata*, must have been effectively litigated by the parties in the process, with effective observance of *due process*. Every citizen is guaranteed at least one day in court.[63]

Now, if, in the balance of the extension of the effects of *res judicata*, the counterweight of security is freedom, then the solution for this extension to be broader (and therefore, security can weigh as much as possible) is the observance of portions of freedoms that cannot be ignored. Thus, if the reach of *res judicata* on a decided prejudicial issue does not represent an undue invasion into the private sphere of the parties and is not a surprise to them, having been effectively litigated about, then it

[63] The confirmation of the legal force of the procedural due process transcends positive law and reaches social relations. The Cambridge dictionary records the curious entry "have your day in court" as an idiomatic expression that goes beyond legal jargon, being applicable in ordinary circumstances of everyday life. The meaning of the expression, according to the lexicon, is: "to get an opportunity to give your opinion on something or to explain your actions after they have been criticised". And the example of application, marked by the power of the court of public opinion, is: *"She was determined to get her day in court and the TV interview would give it to her."*

makes no sense to always and in all cases restrict the authority of *res judicata* to the main claim. Such restriction would be a deficient protection (*untermassverbot*) of *res judicata* and, therefore, unconstitutional, for offending proportionality, as will be demonstrated shortly.

The way out, therefore, is to extend the effects of *res judicata* to decide prejudicial issues, seems to be to ensure that the parties participate in the formation of this incidental decision and also to alert them about the consequences of this participation or non-participation. That is, to inform the parties (either generically, by enacting a legal rule that regulates such extension, or individually, by express warning by the judge in the process) about the extension of the authority of *res judicata* over decided prejudicial issues. Armed with this information, the parties can decide the effort they consider appropriate to expend so that the *res judicata* that is to be formed about the prejudicial issue favours them.

In American jargon, the phrase "one bite of the apple" is often used, meaning that access to jurisdiction is guaranteed once and only once. The bite, however, needs to have been satisfactory. The State cannot prevent the citizen from biting the apple adequately, removing it at the slightest scratch to the skin and, when he tries again, claim that he has already had his bite.

3.3 Fundamental Right to *Res Judicata*: Constitutionally Adequate Protection Between the Prohibition of Excess and the Prohibition of Deficient Protection

Still in the field of "clearing the field" and avoiding misunderstandings, it is necessary to expressly affirm: nothing that is being said relates to the weighing of *res judicata*.

For some years now, in Brazil, positions on the relativisation of *res judicata* have been embroiled in heated discussions about the possibility of, once settled and the rescission period expired, civil *res judicata* being disregarded.[64] The proposal of this work is excluded from this discussion. It is not about disregarding the decision content with the force of *res judicata*, but about delimiting the decision content that can receive this force.

When it is asserted that the extension of *res judicata* is the result of the balance between security and freedom, it is sought, as it is hoped to have been made clear, to question the reasons that would prevent such extension from covering the incidental decisions made in the *iter* decision-making. Security and freedom were

[64] Cf., among all, with comprehensive and rigorous positions, the collective work Didier (2008). Cf., also, the interesting thesis of Antonio do Passo Cabral, who astutely perceives the need to overcome the paradigm of immutability by that of procedural stability, establishing different degrees according to the legal good protected and the possible need for change over time. Cf. Cabral (2012).

weighed in an attempt to find legal grounds that demonstrated the need to cover incidental decisions with the effects of *res judicata*.

The exercise of balancing, carried out here, is *in abstracto*, without examining whether a specific and determined decision can or cannot achieve the effects of *res judicata*. The balancing that was attempted to be exposed above only advances until it is concluded—it is hoped—by the acceptance of the hypothesis proposed in this work, namely, that decisions on preliminary issues can be covered by the authority of *res judicata*, provided that the requirements imposed by freedom are observed.

In fact, *res judicata* not only *can* cover the decided preliminary issues, but *must*. Some argue that the legislator has a certain discretion to decide the scope of shaping *res judicata*.[65,66] However, it is necessary to rethink this premise in light of the fundamental legal theories that underpin the modern Constitutional State.

Now, the ends of the Constitutional State are plural—and, often, antagonistic, as is the case with security and freedom. When it achieves one, the State may be compromising another. In the exercise of abstract balancing between freedom and security in the search for the extension of *res judicata*, it is necessary, therefore, to ensure that, under the pretext of promoting freedom, the State does not excessively expose security. Similarly, when protecting security, a minimum of freedom must always be observed.

Indeed, the principle (or postulate, as H. Ávila demonstrates) of prohibition of excess, sometimes seen as a facet of the principle (or postulate) of proportionality, prohibits excessive restriction of any fundamental right. It is not just about good practice or doctrinal recommendation. It is about seeking parameters for assessing the constitutionality of the State's intervention in procedural fundamental rights.[67] The appropriate balancing of the extension of res judicata is a requirement of the Constitutional State. After all, "[b]eyond other requirements, any restriction or restrictive intervention in a fundamental right only passes the test of constitutionality if it can successively demonstrate that it is suitable for achieving a legitimate end and of superior weight to the fundamental right in question (...)".[68] All the Powers

---

[65] "As long as, attentive to the requirement of security in legal commerce, the need for The stabilisation of litigious or uncertain situations grants the legislator to certain judicial pronouncements this particular authority, which immunises them from further controversies, raises the problem related to the establishment of the conditions whose implementation is to be required for the production of the phenomenon. The law is given the power to use greater or lesser rigour in specifying the requirements necessary for the emergence of res judicata, or – which is to say the same – to restrict or expand its scope of manifestation." Moreira (1967), p. 61. Along the same lines, Mendes (1968), p. 79.

[66] We are not dealing with the different degrees of stability that the legislator can establish for different types of judicial decisions, for which, obviously, there is room for legislative creativity. For, when dealing with materially distinct decisions, it is not necessary for their effects to be identical. Cf. Cabral (2021), pp. 60–61. Cavalcanti (2019), p. 301.

[67] Ávila (2022), p. 188.

[68] Novais (2006), p. 101.

of the Republic are bound by fundamental rights, and their protection is the *raison d'être* of those.[69]

In this sense, both the protection of freedom and that of security cannot be excessive (*untermassverbot*) nor deficient (*ubermassverbot*).

The thesis defended here is that, if the incidental decisions that resolve preliminary issues can be vested with the authority of *res judicata*, provided that the requirements imposed by freedom are observed, then excluding such decisions from that mantle, without sufficient reasons to support such exclusion, implies an excessive protection of freedom or a deficient protection of security. And, therefore, due to its disproportionality, it constitutes unconstitutionality. It is necessary to define the degree of protection constitutionally adequate—neither more, nor less—of the fundamental right to *res judicata*.

It is not, therefore, a matter of legislative policy option to shape *res judicata* from the choice between "a liberal process, in which a restrictive system fundamentally relies on the dispositive principle, and a paternalistic process, in which a comprehensive system will fundamentally seek to avoid disharmony of judgments."[70] It is, rather, about extracting from constitutional values the balancing that best balances them, preserving both, security and freedom, at the same time and to the maximum extent.

In the chapter, it will be demonstrated how the fundamental right to *res judicata* can (or rather, as stated in this topic, *must*) reach decisions on preliminary issues.

References

Alvim AA et al (2016) Comentários ao Código de Processo Civil - Lei n. 13.105/2015. Saraiva, São Paulo

Aristotle (2020) Ética a Nicômaco. Edipro, São Paulo

Ávila H (2021) Teoria da segurança jurídica. JusPodivm, Salvador

Ávila H (2022) Teoria dos princípios. JusPodivm, Salvador

Baini GM (2011) Aspectos da responsabilidade extracontratual da Administração Pública na jurisprudência do Supremo Tribunal Federal – sujeição ativa e passiva. Revista da Associação dos Juízes do Rio Grande do Sul – AJURIS. Ano XXXVIII, n. 122, jun. 2011, p 106

Bauman Z (2017) Liberdade e segurança: um caso de Hassliebe. In: Dessal G, Bauman Z (eds) O retorno do pêndulo: sobre a psicanálise e o futuro do mundo líquido. Zahar, Rio de Janeiro

Cabral AP (2012) Coisa julgada dinâmica: limites objetivos e temporais. Entre continuidade, mudança e transição de posições processuais estáveis. PhD Thesis, Law School at State University of Rio de Janeiro

Cabral AP (2021) Coisa julgada e preclusões dinâmicas: entre continuidade, mudança e transição de posições processuais estáveis. JusPodivm, Salvador

Canaris CW (2003) Direitos fundamentais e direito privado. Almedina, Coimbra

Cavalcanti MA (2019) Coisa julgada & questões prejudiciais - limites objetivos e subjetivos. RT, São Paulo

[69] Canaris (2003), p. 23.

[70] Mendes (1968), p. 120.

Clermont KM (2016) Res Judicata as requisite for justice. Rutgers Univ Law Rev 68:1.067–1.139
Didier F Jr (2008) Relativização da coisa julgada. JusPodivm, Salvador
Didier F Jr, Cabral AP (2018) Coisa julgada e outras estabilidades processuais. JusPodivm, Salvador
Freitas JL (2019) Um polvo chamado autoridade do caso julgado. Revista da Ordem dos Advogados 79(3–4):691–722
Freitas JL, Alexandre I (2015) Código de processo civil anotado. v. 2° - artigos 362.° a 626.°, Almedina, Coimbra
Luhmann N (1980) Legitimação pelo procedimento. Editora Universidade de Brasília, Brasília
Marinoni LG (2018) Coisa julgada sobre questão. Revista dos Tribunais, São Paulo
Marinoni LG, Arenhart SC (2011) Curso de processo civil: processo de conhecimento. 9 ed. rev. e atual. Revista dos Tribunais, São Paulo
Marinoni LG et al (2019) Código de processo civil comentado, 5th edn. Thomson Reuters RT, São Paulo
Mariotti A (2008) Princípio do devido processo legal. 2008. PhD Thesis, Law School at Federal University of Porto Alegre
Mattos SW (2009) Devido processo legal e proteção de direitos. Livraria do Advogado, Porto Alegre
Mendes JC (1963) Manual de processo civil. Coimbra Editora, Lisboa
Mendes JC (1968) Limites objectivos do caso julgado em processo civil. Ática, Lisboa
Moreira JCB (1967) Questões prejudiciais e coisa julgada. 1967. PhD Thesis (Livre-docência in Judiciary Law), Law Schoool at Federal University of Rio de Janeiro
Moreira JCB (2011) Ainda e sempre a coisa julgada. In: Wambier LR, Wambier TAA (coord) Doutrinas essenciais de processo civil, vol 6, p 684 (original In Revista dos Tribunais – RT 416/9 – jun./1970)
Novais JR (2006) Direito fundamentais: trunfos contra a maioria. Coimbra, Coimbra
Oliveira CAA (1996) Formalismo no processo civil. PhD Thesis, Law School at University of São Paulo
Oliveira CAA (2010) Do formalismo no processo civil – proposta de um formalismo-valorativo. Saraiva, São Paulo
Oliveira CAA (2017) O formalismo-valorativo no confronto com o formalismo excessivo. Revista da Faculdade de Direito da UFRGS 26(26), https://doi.org/10.22456/0104-6594.74203. https://seer.ufrgs.br/index.php/revfacdir/article/view/74203. Accessed 06 Aug 2025
Oliveira CAA, Mitidiero D (2012) Curso de processo civil. Atlas, São Paulo
Pinto R (2018a) Caso julgado e autoridade de caso julgado no Código de Processo Civil Português. Revista da Escola da Magistratura do Estado do Rio de Janeiro 20(3):142–158
Pinto R (2018b) Código de Processo Civil anotado. Almedina, Coimbra
Pisani AP (2021) Lezioni di diritto processuale civile. Jovene, Napoli
Savigny FCV (1879) Sistema del derecho romano actual. Tomo V. F. Góngora Y Compañia, Madrid
Schaeffer FA (1984) The great evangelical disaster. Crossway Books, Wheaton
Silva OAB (1979) Limites objetivos da coisa julgada no atual direito brasileiro. Revista de Processo, vol 15
Sousa MT (1983) O objecto da sentença e o caso julgado material (estudo sobre a funcionalidade processual), Lisboa: BMJ 325, pp 125–140
Sousa MT (2017) Preclusão e caso julgado. Lisbon Law Rev LVIII:149–175
Varela JMA et al (1985) Manual de Processo Civil. Coimbra, Coimbra
Vitorelli E (2018) O devido processo legal processual nos precedentes da Suprema Corte dos Estados Unidos: um contributo para a história das garantias processuais. Revista da Faculdade de Direito UFMG, n. 72, Belo Horizonte, pp 187–217
Wasserman R (2004) Procedural due process – a reference guide to the United States Constitution. Greenwood, Connecticut

Chapter 4
Second Outline on the Objective Limits of *Res Judicata*: Defining Criterion – What Becomes Immutable and Undisputable?

Until now, it has been argued that *res judicata* should also cover incidental decisions that, under certain circumstances, resolve prejudicial issues about the main claim, and may even benefit third parties (never harm them).

It was said that the balance between security and freedom requires observance, to the greatest extent: legal certainty (surety and stability), coherence, economy (financial and procedural), efficiency, the unavoidability of jurisdiction, the right to action, the *due process*, the demand, the contradictory, and the broad defence. It was argued that this balance is not just good practice or a space for fundamental legal shaping by the legislator but for constitutionally appropriate protection of the fundamental right to *res judicata.*

It was asserted that the criterion of triple identity erected as the only hypothesis to ascertain the situations in which one demand will be equal to another, for the purposes of the incidence of *res judicata*, does not satisfy the need to balance security and freedom. Instead of this criterion, it was argued that, for the incidence of the principle that prohibits repetition and contradiction of judgements, the *material relationship* judged, and not the procedural one, should be analysed. And, in this case, if the material controversy has been resolved by a judicial decision that has become final, it will be forbidden to relitigate it in court, whether as the main object or as prejudicial.

The resolution of the material controversies effectively litigated is the best criterion to balance security and freedom, adequately shaping the fundamental right to *res judicata*. However, this criterion may still seem excessively imprecise to delimit the scope of *res judicata*.

At this point, it is appropriate to look for *in the process* the delimitation of *res judicata*: What, in a judicial decision, becomes immutable and indisputable? Is it possible to identify in the process the place where *res judicata* is formed?

G. M. Baini, *Objective Limits of Res Judicata*, SpringerBriefs in Law,
https://doi.org/10.1007/978-3-032-07485-0_4

4.1 The Dispute and Its Object

One of the traps from which proceduralists need to dodge in the analysis of the extension of *res judicata* is impermeability.[1] The proposal for defining the limits of *res judicata* should be porous, in the sense that it should allow itself to be penetrated by the material relationship effectively decided in the process. To delimit beforehand and hermetically the *locus* procedural where to inquire the content of *res judicata* tends to the formation of an insufficient proposal.

It is certain that, for methodological rigour, one should always seek the purity of the concepts that are developed on the scientific-doctrinal plane. It is, therefore, understandable the eagerness of proceduralism in identifying at a precise point of the process a place where one can find, with certainty, the decision-making portion endowed with immutability and indisputability. However, the search for the precision of the delimitation of the extension of *res judicata* does not need, necessarily, to confine itself to procedural concepts, as if the need to look at the material law for such delimitation would downgrade proceduralism to some inferior level. On the contrary, the connection with material law enriches the procedural concept of *res judicata*, making it both more precise and more useful. Therefore, it is argued here that the objective limits of *res judicata* are tied to the object and the subjects of the *material* relationship resolved in court.[2] Such conceptualisation shows a greater dedication of the process in fulfilling its mission, that of providing adequate protection of material rights.

Nevertheless, it is possible to better delimit the present proposal, give it "more flesh", so to speak, by working on the procedural concepts traditionally linked to the extension of *res judicata*, either to find in them some auxiliary parameter, or to question the traditional categorical assertions.

The first two, perhaps the main ones, are the concepts of dispute and its object. Now, if *res judicata* is the attribute that makes immutable and indisputable the content of the judgement on the merits, endowing it with obligatory force, and if the judgement on the merits seeks the resolution of the dispute, the decision about the object of the dispute, then it is possible to increase the precision of the contours of *res judicata* from these two concepts.

In an older outline, here invoked only to situate the study, Daniel Mitidiero exemplifies the dispute in Germany in the positions of Karl Heinz Schwab and Walter J. Habscheid, for whom, respectively, the object the dispute would be "the claim properly interpreted in the light of the cause of the claim"[3] or, differently,

[1] About the effort of procedural doctrine in the search for the affirmation of civil procedural law as an autonomous science, cf. Marinoni et al. (2019), item 3.1 "The isolation of civil procedure: from legal isolation to scientific isolation".

[2] Cf. Sects. 3.1.3 and 3.1.3.1, above.

[3] Schwab, K H. El objeto litigioso en el proceso civil. Buenos Aires: EJEA, 1968, p. 244, apud Mitidiero (2006a), p. 52.

would be "*il* Gegenstand, *cioè ça 'cosa' domandata e il* Grund, *cioè la 'causa' della domanda*".[4]

Despite the interesting German view, it is in Italian doctrine that Brazilian proceduralism has sought more inspiration, specifically in the dispute between Francesco Carnelutti and Enrico Tullio Liebman, whose conceptualisations of dispute, object of the dispute, and objective limits of *res judicata* inspired both the Brazilian legislator of 1939 and that of 1973.[5]

Carnelutti conceived the dispute as overflowing the procedural plane, bringing it closer to the social conflict underlying that brought by the parties to the process,[6] while Liebman limited it to what had effectively been transferred by the parties, specifically to the claims they mutually made against each other.[7] From this dispute, one can already foresee the broader or narrower spectrum that the scope of *res judicata* can reach: While for Liebman, *res judicata* is limited to the judgement's ruling, as it would strictly correspond to what is requested by the party, Carnelutti considered that *res judicata* extended even to points of the material legal relationship resolved that were not even raised in the process.[8]

The irreconcilability of these two concepts of dispute and, at the same time, their careless incorporation into the two Civil Procedure Codes of Brazil promulgated in the twentieth century, contributed to the intense doubts and heated discussions about the objective limits of *res judicata* in Brazilian doctrine. Indeed, such discussions develop, perhaps, throughout the procedural doctrine of the Roman-Germanic family systems in Europe and have been for well over a hundred years.[9]

The confusion caused by the lack of a stance on the conceptual content of dispute and its object in legislation directly impacted the inaccuracies related to the objective limits of *res judicata*, revealing that these concepts, *dispute* and *object of the dispute*, contain important keys to understanding the subject of the present study.

[4] Habscheid, W J. L'oggetto del processo nel Diritto Processuale Civile Tedesco, Rivista di Diritto Processuale, v. 35, Padova: CEDAM, 1980, p. 458, apud Mitidiero (2006a), p. 52.

[5] Cf. Silva (1979), p. 124. Mitidiero (2006a), p. 52. According to the last, other eminent Brazilian proceduralists also considered it, such as: Alfredo Buzaid (On the Appeal of Petition in the System of the Civil Procedure Code, 2nd ed., São Paulo: Saraiva, 1956, pp. 102–105); Thereza Arruda Alvim Wambier (Preliminary Issues and the Objective Limits of Res Judicata, São Paulo: RT, 1977, p. 8) and Arruda Alvim (Manual of Civil Procedural Law, v. 1, 7th ed., São Paulo: RT, pp. 434 e 459–460).

[6] As can be inferred, for example, from the statement that perhaps the process can "make the dispute cease, which does not mean to make the conflict cease, which is immanent". Carnelutti (2000). Hence the Italian master was able to conclude by the feasibility of a partial judgment "of the dispute", although it could exhaust the procedural request.

[7] Mitidiero (2006a), pp. 52–54. According to Liebman, dispute would be the "actual or virtual conflict of contradictory requests." (On the sanitising order and the judgment on the merits, In: Studies on Brazilian Civil Procedure, São Paulo: José Bushatski, 1976, p. 122).

[8] Carnelutti F. System of civil procedural law, v. 1, pp. 919–920, apud Silva (1979), pp. 124–127.

[9] As can be seen, for example, in the dispute between Savigny and Chiovenda, which began in the nineteenth century. Cf., below, Sect. 4.2.1 of this study.

Later on, we will return to address them and verify with greater precision their relationship with the extent of the effects of *res judicata*. For now, just as a provocative note, here is a first definition, compatible with the objective extension of *res judicata* supported here: a dispute is the material legal relationship contested in court; the object of the dispute is the underlying good about which the parties dispute legal effects in court.

4.2 Topology of *Res Judicata* from the Perspective of the Judgement: In the Ruling or in the Reasoning?

Another conceptual pair typically procedural that is relevant in the analysis of the extent of the effects of *res judicata* concerns the part of the judgement in which the obligatory force is imposed: Which portion of the judgement contains the attributes of immutability and indisputability? It is precisely from this question that the terminology used to outline the subject of the present study ("extent of the effects of *res judicata*") is revealed: Does *res judicata* restrict itself to the ruling or does it extend to the grounds?

It is natural that the judgement is the place where one asks about the extent of material *res judicata*. After all, it is the decision content that is vested with *res judicata*. And, if it is not "all" the judgement that does so, then one must ask which parts do.

Furthermore, because of the terms used, the legislation lends itself to directing the debate to this place. For example, in articles 580 and 619 of the Portuguese CPC, it is found that the obligatory force imposed with the aim of prohibiting repetition or contradiction refers to the "*decision*" and is found in the "*judgement*". Similarly, articles 503 and 504 of the Brazilian CPC print the force of law to the "*decision*", excluding some parts of the content of the "*judgement*".

But then, what is the *decision* that produces *res judicata*? Which parts of the *judgement* become immutable and indisputable?

First, it is important to recognise that, if there is any margin of legislative autonomy or procedural policy for the shaping of the fundamental right to *res judicata*, some space to legitimately decide whether *res judicata* will be more or less extensive, it is certain that its hard core would be the ruling. That is to say: if it is intended that the legal system operates with a minimum security and that the State contributes minimally to social peace, then at least the content of the ruling needs to become indisputable and immutable.[10]

[10] Demonstrating that all legal systems have a minimum core of protection of res judicata, and this core would be the device of the sentence, cf. Clermont (2016), pp. 1079–1087. A chapter of this article in which the author develops this idea is significantly named "Strong contention: every legal system delivers res judicata's minimal core". On the "so-called guarantee of the essential core of fundamental rights", cf. Sarlet et al. (2020), § 3.9.4.3.

However, the argument of this work is that *res judicata*, as an agent of social peace through the concretisation of security in the Rule of Law, can (*rectius*: should) go beyond this hard core, reaching the decisions about the preliminary issues effectively litigated, without this unjustifiably interfering with the freedom necessary for this same social peace. Now, if it is possible for *res judicata* to also reach questions decided on the way to the production of the ruling, without this expansive effect infringing rights—or that it infringes them only to the extent that can be considered acceptable in view of the benefits to be reaped (and, therefore, a measure *proportional in the strict sense*)—so much the better, in the end, for the Constitutional Rule of Law.[11]

Thus, a first objection to the assertion that *res judicata* is restricted to the ruling of the judgement comes from unsuccessful judgements. A merit decision rejecting the claim has a "negative" content. It does not declare, does not constitute, does not condemn, does not have jurisdictional efficacy of any nature. If *res judicata* were strictly restricted to the ruling, what, in an unsuccessful judgement, would become immutable and indisputable? What legal content would bind the parties?

Now, to extract some legal efficacy from the unsuccessful judgement, obviously, it is necessary to inquire about its grounds. Example: in a re-indicatory action judged unsuccessful, should the defendant be recognised as the owner of the claimed property? And if the basis of the judgement is the insufficiency of evidence (*res judicata secundum eventum litis*), could the plaintiff subsequently file a claim for adverse possession without offending the *res judicata* produced in the previous judgement of dismissal?

The judgement of dismissal can be based on various reasons, both material and procedural. To prevent the court from being put in a position where it is compelled to repeat or risk contradicting the previous judgement, it is always necessary to inquire about the grounds of the unsuccessful judgement[12]—and only they are obstructed. Possible claims about the same life asset that have not been effectively litigated cannot be excluded from the Judiciary's consideration.[13]

On the other hand, let's assume, hypothetically, that *res judicata* cannot be strictly limited to the jurisdictional command contained in the provision ("proceeding" or "not proceeding"), and it is necessary, at least, to analyse the grounds of this

[11] Cf. items 3.2.3 and 3.3 above (fundamental right to constitutionally adequate res judicata).

[12] Savigny (1879), pp. 226–227.

[13] Here we are already stepping on the shifting ground of the so-called "preclusive efficacy of res judicata", just to show that the controversies involving the objective limits of res judicata stem from conceptual problems stemming from a lack of understanding about the need to balance security and freedom optimally. If res judicata were to reach not only what was effectively deduced in court but also what "should have been" deduced (the "deductible"), there would be true excessive protection of the value of security to the detriment of the value of freedom, offending, for example, the principle of demand, of contradiction, of ample defence, etc., at least in relation to the author of a claim judged unfounded. Its application in relation to the defendant in a claim judged founded may merit other considerations in the balance between the values of security and freedom. Despite such considerations overflowing from the present study, the subject will be revisited, slightly, above, in Sect. 4.4.2.

command to understand the immutable and indisputable legal content. In this case, would the provision of a judgement of dismissal in a claim action, read in light of its grounds, by recognising that the defendant meets the requirements to adversely possess the property, make such recognition immutable and indisputable? In a possible action of adverse possession, subsequently filed by the then defendant, could the recognition that he met the requirements to adversely possess the property be questioned again?[14]

As you can see, neither the restriction of *res judicata* to the strict decision-making command contained in the provision, nor its extension to its grounds, even if only to interpret the decision-making command, are sufficient to establish the secure limits of indisputability and immutability.

Another approach would be to resort to another procedural piece, namely the initial petition, specifically the requests made by the plaintiff in the initial petition or, beyond them, the grounds on which they are formulated (in good rigour: the cause of the request). Thus, one would inquire what request was judged to proceed/not proceed, and on what bases it was presented, so that the legal content covered by *res judicata* could be identified.

Although useful, this integration between judgement and initial petition does not solve all problems, as will be discussed later in this work.[15] However, it is advisable to try to identify a possible origin for the conflict between the positions that advocate the restriction of *res judicata* to the provision or its extension to the grounds—and try to contribute to repositioning this controversy.

It is therefore concluded that the provision, alone, can never contain all of *res judicata*, and it is always necessary to resort to the grounds to investigate what has binding force. The question, then, is another: Do the grounds also make *res judicata*? or do they only serve to interpret the provision for the purpose of defining the material content of the *res judicata* produced?

4.2.1 Pandectism Between Savigny and Chiovenda

After a long period of political and legal atomisation in medieval Europe, gradually succeeded by unification and formation of modern states, jurists found themselves with the enormous burden of finding systemic solutions to assist in this transition. Acting as true architects of their legal systems, jurists produced various answers to

[14] It is known that adverse possession can be argued in defence, as assured by Summary n. 237 of the STF. However, it is also known that property could not be granted to the defendant who opposes it due to the specificities of the special rite to which the adverse possession action is subjected, justified to protect the interests of third parties, such as the Union, the State, the Municipality and the neighbours, who need to have their "freedom" (in the terms described in Sect. 3.2.2.2, above) safeguarded, under penalty of *ubermassverbot* and *üntermassverbot* freedom.

[15] Cf. Sect. 4.3, below.

the problem of the legitimacy of coercive imposition by the State—that is, the legitimacy of the Rule of Law.

For example, the so-called Exegetical School, predominant in Revolutionary France, advocated the legitimacy of Law in the "popular will", in representative democracy manifested by the National Assembly.[16] But, on the other side of the Rhine, the most sophisticated thinkers of the so-called Historical School of Law[17] were not satisfied with legitimisation by *auctoritas* popular, seeking to recognise, in the legal phenomenon, a historical–cultural character. The legitimacy of Law was not in pure reason (the prerogative of scholastic natural law), refuted by the emergence of sociological positivism, nor in the political authority of the legislator (as propagated by French Exegesis), as this manifested a risk of incongruity between Law and Justice.

According to Savigny, one of the main exponents of the Historical School, the legitimacy of law was based "on the history and evolution of each people, as well as on the common traditions of all humanity".[18] Starting from these two foundations, Savigny sought to understand his time, the *zeitgeist,* drawing a historical line (in fact, a complex plot) to his contemporary Germany from the ancient Romanist tradition, of which he was considered an heir.

Savigny's monumental work, *System des Heutigen Römiscen Rechts* (1840), exactly represents this spirit, as its significant title reveals. Through it, and imbued with that mission, Savigny sought to update the *Pandecta*[19]—the part of the *Corpus Iuris Civilis* corresponding to the glosses and comments of the ancient Roman jurists, the *doctrine* Roman, so to speak—to develop the legal system that best met the two pillars he identified as the foundation of legitimacy for Law: the historical evolution of the German people inserted in what he considered to be the common traditions of the Western world.

Applying this methodology to the doctrine of *res judicata,* Savigny interpreted the part of the *Pandecta* entitled *"De exceptione rei judicatae*" *(Digesta,* Book XLIV, Tit. 2), seeking to demonstrate, from this portion of ancient Roman Law, that,

---

[16] Cf. among all, Neves (2010), School of Exegesis.

[17] Cf. among all, Neves (2010), Historical School of Law.

[18] This is evident, especially in the first and last pages, in Savigny's response to Thibaut when, writing against the codification of German law by the a priori and idealistic apprehension of law—that is, without connection to time and space—, he publishes, in 1814, the famous text On the vocation of our time for legislation and the science of law. The passage in parentheses is a paraphrase of a quote from Savigny (System of today's Roman Law) made by Neves (2010), Historical School of Law, p. 205.

[19] Hence the name of this movement inserted in the context of the Historical School called pandectism. Cf. Wieacker (1980), pp. 430–459, for whom the main pandectists would be Hugo, Savigny and Putcha, although in the latter, possibly due to the influence of romanticism (Wieacker highlights Thibaud's friendship with Schiller and Goethe), historicism deviates, to some extent, towards conceptualism, possibly leading to the dispute between Romanism and Germanism in which Chiovenda is involved, as will be demonstrated later.

in the German judgement, not only the ruling but also *"los motivos tienen la autoridad de la cosa juzgada"*.[20]

Another jurist of great stature might perhaps be belatedly inserted into the Historical School. However, with a difference: while Savigny considered it necessary to insert current times into the tradition from which they emerged, for Giuseppe Chiovenda, the legitimacy of Law seems to lie more in pure tradition than in its updating. Engaged in a personal project of reforming Italian procedural law almost a century later, Chiovenda fought against the doctrine of his time, refuting its dogmatic character by distancing it from "pure Roman law", as if the legal institutions of Rome were the "correct Law", the paradigm to be followed. Neutralising the Roman concepts in relation to culture and adopting a conceptualist stance, Chiovenda is said to have claimed that "everything that is good in modern procedure is Roman and everything that is bad constitutes its degeneration".[21]

Applying this conception to the doctrine of *res judicata*, the Italian proceduralist set about "discovering the Roman concept" of *res judicata*, restrictively linked, according to him, to the claim and the ruling of the judgement,[22] in direct opposition to Savigny's doctrine.

Chiovenda condemned what he considered to be scholastic tendencies of medieval Italian procedural law, which had preserved, from the Roman *res judicata*, only the name or little more, as it had ignored that the Romanistic essence of the *res judicata* was linked only to conviction or acquittal, without consideration for the judge's reasoning or what he considered to be mere *"provvedimenti direttivi della lite"*. For him, such doctrinal error would result from a seduction by the logicism that shone in that historical context, leading the *"processualisti loicizzanti"* to see in the judgement the conclusion of a syllogism (or a *"ossatura silogistica del giudizio"*). All this would have led the doctrine to mistakenly associate *res judicata* with the logical reasoning of the judge and, thus, with the resolution of preliminary issues contained in the part of the judgement topographically located outside the ruling.[23]

Under the claim of rescuing the Roman concept, Chiovenda sought to disconnect *res judicata* from the judge's reasoning, linking it exclusively to the legal protection of the State (the conviction, declaration, constitution, mandate, or execution)—that

[20] This is the subtitle given to §§ CCXCI, CCXCII, CCXCIII and CCXCIV of the consulted work: Savigny (1879), pp. 223–258. It is known that, despite the huge influence of Savigny's doctrine on German law (and also on the entire family of Roman-Germanic legal systems), especially on substantive law, the ZPO did not adopt the extension of the effects of res judicata to the reasons, advocated by the learned jurist.

[21] Chiovenda G. Romanesimo e germanesimo, In: Saggi di diritto processualle civile (1900–1930), pp. 181–224, apud Marinoni (2018), pp. 145–146.

[22] Chiovenda G. Sulla cosa giudicata. In: Saggi di diritto processualle civile , v. 2, p. 399 and ss. Chiovenda G. Cosa giudicata e preclusione. In: Saggi di diritto processualle civile, v. 3, pp. 231 and ss. apud Marinoni (2018), pp. 145ss.

[23] CHIOVENDA. Sulla cosa giudicata…, pp. 401–402, apud Marinoni (2018), pp. 147–148. This is also the view of Moreira (1967), pp. 87–89.

is, to the judgement of the claim's validity or invalidity.[24] According to the Italian proceduralist, the resolution of the "logical issues that arise in the process", contained in the judgement or in interlocutory decisions, related to "procedural or substantial issues", would not be reached by *res judicata*, but would have a "more limited effectiveness, imposed by requirements of order and security of the process development", namely, "the preclusion of the ability to renew the same issue *in the same process*".[25]

For Chiovenda, Savigny's proposal to attribute *res judicata* authority to the reasons for the judgement confused the statehood of the jurisdictional act, which, in his opinion, focused exclusively on the act of accepting or rejecting the main claim. That is to say, the state element, which enforces the concrete will of the law by granting or denying the good of life claimed by the plaintiff, would be an act of will of the State—the Roman judgement would express the sovereignty of the State and the power of the judge to state the law. What preceded this act, even if it involved, occasionally, decisions, would represent the merely logical element—an element to which the Romans would never have looked—a set of observations, reasoning, and declarations, which represented no more than "*premesse logiche della emanazione dell'atto di volontà*".[26]

That is, for this great influencer of the Roman-Germanic procedural doctrine of the twentieth century, the resolution of preliminary issues, whether in the body of the judgement or in interlocutory decisions, consisted of a mere syllogistic premise of the judicial reasoning to judge the main issue, suffering only the preclusive effect of preventing its rediscussion *in the process*, but not the effect of *res judicata*, with binding force *outside the process*. On the contrary, for him, the preliminary issues decided in one process could always be rediscussed in another, with a single exception: when, *by legal provision or by the will of the parties*, the preliminary issue was decided at the level of an incidental declaratory action, then it would be vested with *res judicata*, as such a decision would be a true judgement, resolving an express and specific claim relating to a good of life different from that which constitutes the main claim.[27]

However, the "reasons" to which Savigny attributes *res judicata* authority bear no resemblance to the logical reasoning that Chiovenda so combatively argues to exclude from the effects of immutability and indisputability.

Savigny distinguishes "reasons" from "simple reasons", or objective reasons from subjective reasons.[28] While simple reasons (or subjective reasons) have to do with the judge's inner conviction, "*influyen sobre el espíritu* del juez",[29] Your thinking, your preferences, the decision-making valuations (*cognitio*) that trigger

[24] Marinoni (2018), p. 149.

[25] Chiovenda, Cosa giudicata…, p. 267, apud Marinoni (2018), pp. 149–50.

[26] Chiovenda, Cosa giudicata…, p. 256, apud Marinoni (2018), p. 155.

[27] Chiovenda, Cosa giudicata…, p. 268, apud Marinoni (2018), p. 150.

[28] Savigny (1879), p. 223 ss.

[29] Savigny (1879), p. 229.

judgement (*iudicium*), the motives (objectives) are the legal premises (not merely logical) on which the judgement is based, or "*las partes constitutivas de las relaciones juridicas*".[30] It is as if Savigny dissects, so to speak, a legal relationship into sub-relationships. For example, a credit relationship may derive from a contractual relationship. In resolving the latter to decide on the former, the judge would be establishing "objective motives" for judgement about the credit relationship. Indeed, when Savigny attributes the authority of *res judicata* to the motives, he is referring to the "*resoluciones de derecho*" that culminate in the act imposed on the defendant: his conviction or acquittal.[31]

Thus, in a maintenance action, the defendant's paternity would be an objective motive, while the intensity of the sense of family responsibility and the consideration of the economic condition of the parties to estimate the value of the pension would be subjective motives. On the first, Savigny would consider there to be *res judicata*. On the latter, not.[32]

---

[30] Savigny (1879), p. 229.

[31] Savigny (1879), p. 228.

[32] With another purpose and using another terminology, Michele Taruffo addresses the same phenomenon when distinguishing between decision-making reasoning and justificatory reasoning. The former "is the procedure by which the judge formulates the final decision, through a concatenation of choices, of hypotheses dismissed or confirmed, of changes that occur in the course of the process, of elaboration and valuation that culminate in the final decision", while the latter "is the reasoning with which the judge, after having formulated the final decision [or before—in this context this temporal discussion is not very relevant], organises a justificatory reasoning in which he exposes the 'good reasons' on the basis of which his decision should be accepted as valid and shareable." Decision-making reasoning, close to the context of discovery, "unfolds over time, implies the synthesis of various factors, proceeds by abductions and by trial and error, traverses paths that are later abandoned, includes the influence of psychological and ideological factors, implies value judgements and may also involve the participation of several people, as occurs in all cases where the decision is given by a panel of judges. On the other hand, the judicial equivalent of the context of justification, i.e., the motivation of the sentence, has different characteristics: (...) it can be the work of people different from those who formulated the decision and – usually – of only one of these; it does not aim to make choices, but to show that the choices made were 'good'; it has an argumentative and not heuristic structure; it has a justificatory function; it is a 'discourse' – and therefore a linguistic entity – and not a psychological iter; it is based on arguments with potentially intersubjective validity; it is logically structured; it may include deductive and inductive inferences, but not abductive ones, and so on." Insisting on the irrelevance of the judge's "internal" reasoning for the motivation of the sentence (and hence the link with the terminology used by Savigny, the motives), and proving the impossibility that such "subjective motives" (to use Savigny's terminology) cannot be vested with the authority of res judicata, Taruffo concludes: "What is asked of the judge is not his psychoanalysis or self-analysis: it is asked, however, that he expose arguments on the basis of which the external observer (the parties, the lawyers, the other judges, the public opinion) can verify that that decision is logically and legally founded. (...) it is assumed that he has rationally formulated the decision instead of throwing the dice or surrendering to the inscrutable inner impulses of his soul. However, we must not forget that, in reality, we do not know and cannot know anything about what the actual 'real reasons' were that determined the decision and to what extent a decision can be well justified regardless of the way in which the judge came to formulate it." Taruffo (2014), pp. 16–19. Cf., also, in the same work and extensively, about the decision-making reasoning of the justificatory discourse, pp. 191–276.

Therefore, despite the terminological confusion, it is clear that Savigny is referring to preliminary issues—or, more precisely, to *points* of preliminary issues, as he does not restrict the authority of *res judicata* only to the "motives" actually litigated by the parties, with which one cannot agree—that precede and condition the judgement.[33] The motives on which Savigny considers the authority of *res judicata* to fall are the "*consideraciones que influyen* [rectius: condition] *sobre la determinacion del juez, determinacion que se traduce en la práctica por una condena ó una absolucion*"[34] Clearly, therefore, Savigny's "motives" are not mere logical reasoning, but *points* of preliminary issues, which transform into *questions* when disputed.[35]

In the end, the German ZPO of 1877 did not accommodate Savigny's theory of *res judicata* on the motives,[36] also influencing the Italian legislator, who later changed the guideline previously adopted in the *Codice* of 1865,[37] a guideline closely followed in Brazil and Portugal.

4.2.2 *(Follows: Topology of* Res Judicata *in the Judgement) Repositioning the Controversy: Ontological Indistinction in the Decision-Making Reasoning and in the Decision of Both the Main Issue and the Preliminary One*

Chiovenda and Savigny were chosen as representatives of a myriad of jurists who adopt one of the two positions about the extent of the effects of *res judicata* in relation to its location in the judgement: restricted to the ruling or extended to its foundations.

Both Savigny and Chiovenda have good arguments. The divergence between these giants seems to be, however, merely conceptual. If the meanings of the words used by the authors were the same, a convergence would be possible.

Indeed, there is a syllogistic chain in the decision-making reasoning. To judge, the judge indeed deduces conclusions from premises. To intend to stabilise with the force of *res judicata* all the syllogistic deductions made by the judge seems

[33] To try to distinguish such motives from those on which res judicata does not fall and, with this, to try to avoid the confusions, apparently without much success, of which Chiovenda fell victim, Savigny uses another word—"elementos"—to refer to the elements of the legal relations disputed in court. Cf. pp. 228–229.

[34] Savigny (1879), p. 229.

[35] Cf. Sect. 3.1.4, supra, about point and prejudicial question.

[36] The main reason that would have deterred the German legislator from Savigny's theses would be the controversy about the identification of res judicata with the truth—whether as a presumption or as a fiction, initially advocated by Ulpiano (embodied in the Latin brocard *res judicata pro veritate accipitur*) and, modernly, by Pothier, whose influence ended up expressly assumed in the Code Napoleon—a topic so dear and so heatedly debated among the German philosophers of the nineteenth century. Cf. Marinoni (2018), pp. 163–165 and Taruffo (1972), pp. 274 ss.

[37] Taruffo (1972), p. 280, footnote n. 172.

undesirable, either for trivialising one of the most relevant institutes of the judicial process, or for not producing a useful enough result to overcome the objections of individual freedom against undue state interventions.[38]

However, when the judge deduces conclusions from the premises, not his reasoning, but the conclusion seems to have a different nature from that of mere logicism. It is a decision. Notably in judicial decision-making reasoning, and specifically in the modern theory of sceptical-moderate interpretation of the so-called Genoese realism,[39] the judge reasons and decides to apply the law to the concrete case. He reasons, yes, but also decides. The interpretative process, in this view, is logical-argumentative: logical, because he needs to identify the possible meanings of the text and the norm interpreted, delimiting the interpretative possibilities within the semantic reach of the interpreted text; argumentative, because he needs to give the reasons why he chose the meaning he considered appropriate for the concrete case under judgement. And once the *interpretation-process* is completed, the *interpretation-result* is obtained. That is, the result of the interpretative process is always decisional. It is on the result, and not on the process, that there is a need and justification for the stabilisation conferred by *res judicata*.

On the other hand, the criticisms of the syllogistic conception of decision-making reasoning when applied to the theory of judicial decision are not ignored.[40] However, recognising the restrictions that this conception suffers from, it is undeniable that, from a certain perspective, decision-making reasoning— including judicial—has a syllogistic scope. And this scope that is sought to be highlighted here is seen when it is perceived that, to reach the ruling, the judge goes through a path of successive decisions, as many as are the issues that the parties present to him. Around the "final syllogism", there is a series of "instrumental syllogisms" (*Hilfsyllogismen*), concatenated in such a way that their respective conclusions constitute the premises of the final syllogism.[41] Such instrumental conclusions, however, produce conclusions in their own right. That is, when deciding on legal effects about which the parties present doubt, effectively litigating about it, and which condition the judgement of the claim, the judge simultaneously resolves the issue entirely and partially resolves the dispute. They establish, at the same time, conclusions (regarding the resolved issue) and premises (regarding the main claim).[42]

Thus, if the decision-making reasoning is done several times to judge the main claim, there are several decisions resulting from the interpretative process. And as many times as *res judicata* can occur as there are decisions produced, that is, the issues resolved, in the sense attributed above in the text.

---

[38] Cf. supra Sects. 3.2.2.2.1 and 3.2.2.2.2, in which such "freedom objections" are described.

[39] Cf. above all Tarello (1980). Chiassoni (2007). Guastini (2011).

[40] Cf. above all Taruffo (2014), pp. 147–163.

[41] Rosenberg-Schwab, Zivilprocessrecht, 10, Aufl., München, 1969, p. 686; Engish, Logische Studien, p. 16; Manestrina, La pregiudiziale nel processo civile, Vienna, 1904, p. 41; Rigaux, La nature du contrôle de la Cour de cassation, Bruxelles, 1966, p. 39. All apud Taruffo (2014), p. 148.

[42] Taruffo (2014), pp. 24–25.

The provision of the judgement (the conviction or acquittal) can indeed be seen as the result of an interpretative process similar, from a certain perspective, to the syllogism. Perhaps it is, indeed, more than a syllogism, as Chiovenda wanted. But this is irrelevant when it is realised that the judicial decision on which *res judicata* can occur is not limited to the final conclusion regarding the main request—the conviction or acquittal. If the judicial decision can actually result from several interpretative processes, producing several interpretative results, then all of them are individually susceptible to being vested with the authority of *res judicata*, provided that, as has been argued since the introduction of this study, the requirements imposed by freedom against excessive state intervention are observed. In this sense, the judgement is not just a simple syllogism between the law (major premise) and the fact (minor premise). However, it can be understood as the result of a sequence of heuristic or constructive processes—better said, interpretative processes (logical-argumentative, as said)—all similar to each other and ordered to resolve a main issue. There is no ontological distinction in the decision-making process that resolves the main issue and the preliminary issues.

The divergence between Chiovenda and Savigny—or between the restriction of *res judicata* to the provision and its extension to the grounds—can be overcome if it is possible to identify, in the decision-making reasoning taken by the judge to resolve the preliminary issues, characteristics similar to those of the process of judicial resolution of the main issue. This is what has been attempted here.

4.2.3 *(Follows: Topology of* Res Judicata *in the Judgement) Repositioning the Controversy: Which Grounds Make* Res Judicata*?* Res Judicata *on a Decision that Resolves Preliminary Issues*

The difficulties in reconciling those who advocate the extension of *res judicata* to the grounds with those who restrict it to the provision can already be overcome by the definition that *not all* grounds can be reached by *res judicata*. But *some* can.

As has been argued since the introduction, hoping that it is clear by now, the decisions that the judge makes to resolve preliminary issues, provided they are effectively litigated (with real opportunity to allege and prove) by the parties, can (*rectius*: should) stabilise.

The resolution of an issue also constitutes a jurisdictional decision, because it also responds, in a sense, to an action (of substantive law)[43] that could be called a "preliminary action", formulated by one of the parties (either the plaintiff or the defendant) in the process in which the main action is formulated.

Applying this reasoning to one of the numerous examples above (but it could be applied to any of them and to many others), one can imagine the case of the plaintiff

[43] Cf. Silva (2006), pp. 19–22. Mitidiero (2006b).

who asks the defendant for alimony claiming to be his son. Now, the request is for alimony. But one of the *essential facts* from which the plaintiff derives the legal effects he intends is his filiation in relation to the defendant (another could be, for example, the defendant's financial ability and the plaintiff's need).[44] If the plaintiff claims that he is a son and the defendant does not deny it, paternity is a point that the judge assumes in his decision. However, if the defendant denies it, this point becomes an issue and the judge will need to decide. The way the judge decides it *conditions* the judgement of the request: if paternity is rejected, the alimony is prejudiced; if recognised, they are admissible.

Two aspects highlighted in this example deserve attention.

First, the same link in the chain of the judge's reasoning to examine the main request can be a point or an issue, depending on the existence or not of controversy about it. Second, if there is no controversy, there is not, properly, *decision*—whatever is there is is mere logical chaining (or better, one could say, mere *non-decisional conditioning premise* of the decision). On the other hand, if there is controversy, there is a decision. Why wouldn't this decision be vested with the effects of *res judicata*?

In addition, above we spoke of "action of substantive law" and "essential facts". These concepts are directly linked to a next pair that also deserves to be observed so that clearer outlines can be found about the object of *res judicata*. Action of substantive law and essential facts refer to request and cause of action.

4.3 Topology of *Res Judicata* from the Perspective of the Initial Petition: Claim and Cause of Action

Just as with the device/foundation binomial, the claim/cause of claim binomial, although it does not lend itself to the precise definition of where *res judicata* can be identified, helps to contrast the limits, contributing to this desideratum.

In fact, it is in the connection of one binomial with another that things start to become less confusing. An example given above reveals the insufficiency of restricting *res judicata* to the device—or even to the foundations—and illustrates the need to connect the judgement to the initial petition to better visualize the scope of *res judicata*. In the case of an unsuccessful proprietary action, could it be concluded that the defendant is the owner of the claimed property? Wouldn't it be necessary to connect the judgement (whether just its device or this interpreted in light of its foundations) to the claims, inquiring about the very *existence of a claim* (actually, some kind of counterclaim) of property recognition by the defendant in order to consider the formation of *res judicata* in this sense? More than that: as established by art. 322, § 2°, of the Brazilian CPC, "the interpretation of the claim will consider the set

[44] The binomial necessity/possibility is enshrined both in Portuguese legislation (Art. 2004 of the Portuguese Civil Code) and in Brazilian legislation (Art. 1694, § 1, of the Brazilian Civil Code).

of the postulation", it cannot be done in isolation. It is, therefore, essential to analyse the claim in the context of the initial petition— which includes the cause of the claim.

Therefore, it is clear that the claim and the cause of the claim must be taken into account when inquiring about the objective limits of *res judicata*.

The relationship between claim and cause of claim is widely explored in doctrine and overflows the limits of this work, so it is not intended, here, to develop it. One point, however, stands out, namely, an important connection between *cause of claim* and *preliminary issue*: the cause of claim, when directly contested by the defendant, constitutes the preliminary issue par excellence.

In the classic example of a maintenance action, while the claim pertains to the payment of a credit, suppose that the cause of claim is, hypothetically, the defendant's paternity and the claimant's economic need. Both can be questioned by the defendant. In this case, they become a preliminary issue to the main claim, giving rise to the possibility of a decision with the force of *res judicata*.

Regarding the stabilisation of legal effects, there are two important distinctions between these two causes of claim.

One, slightly more perceptible, concerns the temporal limits of *res judicata*. While paternity represents a perennial phenomenon (as the relationship of filiation, at least the natural/biological one, does not change over time), economic need is greatly volatile (as at one moment it can be great, at another small). Therefore, the claimant's economic need is susceptible to review, remaining, if it is the case to stabilise it through a specific incidental decision, under the effect of the *rebus sic stantibus* clause.[45]

However, as already stated, this is a problem about the *temporal* limits of *res judicata*. Strange, therefore, to the present study, which focuses on its *objective* limits.

For what matters here, it is enough to say that, in the example of the maintenance action, the *res judicata* that can be produced about the economic need alleged by the claimant and possibly contested by the defendant, can be objectively recognised, but will surely be temporally questionable.

The second important distinction between the two causes of claim of the hypothetical maintenance action described above impacts on the definition of the objective extent of *res judicata*, so it is explored.

---

[45] Indeed, as proposed by Antonio do Passo Cabral, in contemporary society, the understanding of stability is less dense than it once was, demanding more space for change (one can remember, once again, Bauman and his "liquid modernity"). Thus, the Brazilian proceduralist proposes, "instead of working with the concept of 'security as immutability', we will try to base the model of stabilities on the concept of legal continuity in which the stability achieved has a prima facie force that guarantees its permanence, but does not prevent its modification. Even though, in this way, changes continue to be exceptional, all procedural acts, and with them all judicial decisions, must be understood as essentially mutable, that is, stable si et in quantum the elements and circumstances that led to that result are maintained." Cabral (2012), p. 29. In this author's proposal, it is always necessary, therefore, to admit the possibility of reviewing the res judicata, provided that the factual-legal conditions on which it is given are changed. Cf. Cabral (2021), pp. 301–401.

Unlike economic need, paternity represents a legal relationship conditioning the maintenance claim that could be the subject of an autonomous action (paternity investigation action), thus constituting an example of what Andrea Proto Pisani calls a "fact-right" (*fatto-diritto*).[46] Therefore, being a cause of claim that could be placed in the position of a claim, it would represent, for the Italian author, a preliminary issue capable of being covered by material *res judicata*. The stability formed on the economic need of the alimentary, however, could always be problematised, so, as it relates to facts, and not properly to a stabilisable material legal relationship, it would be limited to formal *res judicata endoprocessual*), as it would relate to *facts*.

There are causes of claim, therefore, that are limited to *facts,* and cannot, from this perspective, be reached by material *res judicata*.[47]

Luiz Guilherme Marinoni, however, seems to deepen this debate, arguing that the extension of *res judicata* to preliminary issues could have an even greater reach. Although he does not affirm material *res judicata* on facts, for him, the decision on a preliminary issue can relate to a cause of claim that is not susceptible to composing an autonomous action and, still, be covered by *res judicata*, as in the case of "a fact to which a legal effect can be associated".[48]

For example, for the purposes of civil liability in a car accident, driving above the speed limit can be a fact attributed to the defendant associated with the legal effect *fault*. In a compensation action brought by the victim, a judicial decision that recognises that the defendant was driving above the speed limit and, therefore, negligently caused an accident, can be reached by the effects of the *res judicata*? Assuming there are multiple victims in the same accident, an affirmative answer to this question would allow the others to take advantage of the decision that recognised the common defendant's guilt.

Marinoni's position can be defended more comfortably when the authority of *res judicata* is attributed not to the fact recognised by the judge (driving above the speed limit), but to its legal effect (guilt). In other words, the discussion is indeed about the extent of the effects of *res judicata* on the resolution of a preliminary issue, since an issue always involves factual and legal elements.[49]

---

[46] Pisani A P (2002), Lezioni di diritto processuale civile. Napoli: Jovene, p. 58, apud Marinoni (2016), p. 98.

[47] Cf. footnote n. 29 of the Chap. 2 of this work.

[48] Here one could add another tangled controversy in which it is not intended to enter, which is why this note is not in the text of the work. But it is worth problematising: could the authority of res judicata rest on the recognition of a fact? This doubt touches on the almost metaphysical discussion about the basis of res judicata as a "presumption of truth" or "fiction of truth" of what the judge establishes in the sentence as a basis to justify the effects of res judicata. The problem of truth is one of the most intricate concepts of Philosophy. And when it encounters Law, there will hardly be unanimity. Regarding res judicata, the Brazilian Code of Civil Procedure provides that the facts on which the sentence is pronounced do not make res judicata—art. 504, II. On the subject, cf. Macêdo (2016).

[49] Cf. Neves (2010), A distinção entre a questão-de-facto e a questão-de-direito e a competência do Supremo Tribunal de Justiça como tribunal de "revista" (Digesta). Alvim (2022). Anyway, it would still be worth provoking: does the legal effect resulting from a fact (guilt resulting from speed at

The example can be complicated. Imagine a motor vehicle liability action in which the plaintiff alleges that the defendant was driving at high speed when he negligently collided with his vehicle. The defendant, in turn, claims that (i) the vehicle was driven by an unauthorised third party, (ii) who, however, was driving within the speed limit and with all the precautions that could legitimately be expected, (iii) the vehicle hit is not owned by the plaintiff, and (iv) the collision was the result of an abrupt deviation by a third party who crossed the road in the wrong direction. Well, there are at least four issues to be resolved before the judgement of the claim's success or failure, all raised by the defendant as facts that prevent, modify or extinguish the plaintiff's right: (i) authorship of the damage, (ii) fault of the offender, (iii) absence of damage to the plaintiff, (iv) causal link.

It can be seen, therefore, that the claim/cause of action binomial must be expanded to also consider the *defendant's defence*, in order to correctly assess the extent of the effects of *res judicata*.[50]

In addition, there is another link that assists in defining the scope of *res judicata*, which connects not the judgment to the initial petition (and defence), but the claim to the cause of action, referring to those causes of action that could constitute independent actions, pointed out by Proto Pisani as *fatto-diritto*, as mentioned above.

According to the good technique used in the drafting of art. 581, n. 3 and 4, c/c art. 5, n. 1, both of the Portuguese CPC, "claim" is the legal effect sought by the party, while "cause of action" are the essential legal facts from which the claim proceeds.

Now, when the plaintiff who asks for alimony alleges that the defendant is his father, inserting this link in the logical chain that develops to the claim, even if he does not ask for a declaration of paternity, he is asserting the production of a legal effect—a kinship relationship. This effect is distinct from that resulting from the alimony claim—the establishment of a monthly credit in his favour. The lack of a claim about paternity derives from the presumption, assumed by the plaintiff, that this fact is uncontroversial. The distinction between the *claim* for paternity and the *cause of action* for paternity is accidental. However, the defendant may allege the contrary in defence, making this *fatto-diritto* controversial and, therefore, capable of being resolved with the force of *res judicata*.

There is, therefore, a potential ontological similarity between the claim, the cause of action and the facts alleged in defence by the defendant:[51] sometimes, the

---

the wheel) relate to the "truth of the facts", as provided for in art. 504, II, of the CPC (and, therefore, does not make res judicata) or to the "prejudicial question", as provided for in art. 503, § 1, of the Brazilian CPC (and, therefore, can make res judicata)?

[50] As the Latin brocard says, *reus in exceptione actor est.* It is no coincidence that the principle of demand shapes the matter brought to court in the initial petition and in the defence. Cf. art. 5, n. 1, 336 and 573, all of the portuguese CPC. The interesting definition of the object of the process contained in the ELI/UNIDROIT Rules contemplates this conception, as can be seen from its art. 23, n. 1: "The object of the process is delimited by the claims and defences put forward by the parties in their pleadings".

[51] Pisani (2021), p. 328: *"il petitum della domanda pregiudiziale è parte della causa petendi o fatto impeditivo, modificativo, estintivo della domanda dipendente."*

cause of action and the grounds of defence will be, in themselves, capable of occupying the position of claim, provided that another legal fact is alleged to support it (example: biological descent or socio-affective filiation) or that it is positioned in the initial petition, and not in the defence (e.g. economic non-necessity of the alimented or denial of paternity).

It is in this sense that we talk about the approximation between claims and causes of action. And it is in this sense that it can be said that the cause of action can contain as many "material law actions" as there are preliminary issues (controversial points) raised in the process for examination of the final claim.

After all that has been said about the topology of *res judicata*, both from the perspective of the judgement and the initial petition, it is necessary to recognise that the attempt to identify a place in the process where the objective limits of *res judicata* can be found contributes, but does not completely solve the problem.

Instead, the claims and causes of action, as well as the defence allegations, are more relevant in defining the limits of the judicial relief demanded. That is, they establish the object of the dispute, giving contours to the claim that will be decided and on which, after all, *res judicata* will be produced.

4.4 (Again:) The Dispute and Its Object: Main and Preliminary Issues in Defining the Limit of Material *Res Judicata*

It is hoped to have demonstrated, with the two topics above, that the effects of *res judicata* that make the legal content decided by the judge immutable and indisputable cannot be limited either to the judgment or to the initial petition.

In truth, if one is to look for some locus in the procedural process from which the objective limits of *res judicata* can be delimited, the best thing to do is to replace the claim/cause of action and ruling/grounds binomials with two others: *res judicata* can be identified, first with the "claim/ruling" (main issue); and then with the "controversial cause of action[52]/decisive grounds" (preliminary issue).

What the parties request and argue shapes the claim upon which the judge will deliver a judgement. The claim, in this respect, is not merely the request nor solely the defence, but includes what the parties argue to request and to defend themselves. What the parties do, strictly speaking, when outlining the claim, arguing and requesting, is to bring to the court the points of the substantive legal relationship about which they seek jurisdiction. And it is on these points that the *res judicata* is formed.

[52] From the Latin perspective that reus in exceptione actor est, the defence allegations that represent impeding, modifying or extinguishing facts of the plaintiff's right can be considered, mutatis mutandis, "causes of action" of the defence. Cf. art. 23, n. 1, of the ELI/UNIDROIT Rules.

The contentious object is not limited to the plaintiff's request. The allegations conditioning the request or its rejection (that is, the cause of the request alleged by the plaintiff and the facts impeding, modifying, and extinguishing the plaintiff's right alleged by the defendant) can also be disputed, thus expanding the contentious object. After all, would the contentious object be only the compensation for contractual non-compliance, or, if disputed, is it also the validity of the contract? Would the contentious object be only the right to compensation for the car accident or, if disputed, is it also the existence of the damage, the driver's fault and the causal link between his driving and the damage? The contentious object is, therefore, the good of life about which the parties dispute in the process. Everything that the parties litigate reveals the legal uncertainty for whose resolution the parties resort to the State-Judge. If there is no dispute, judicial intervention infringes individual freedom. On the other hand, if there is a dispute, and the parties submit it to the judge, a judgement that does not resolve it does not represent adequate state protection.

The substantive legal relationship about which the parties dispute represents the object of the dispute,[53] therefore delimiting the jurisdictional protection sought and, moreover, the *res judicata*.

When the judge delivers a judgement on a maintenance action, what is at stake is not only the right to maintenance, but the entire substantive legal relationship in which maintenance may be due. The limits of the *res judicata* produced in the context of this action, however, do not exceed, but also do not fall short of what the parties effectively litigate. The parties' allegations (paternity and the economic need of the maintenance recipient, for example) can also be part of the dispute over which the judge will have to decide. If they are part of it, there is no reasonable reason why the decision that resolves it should not produce *res judicata*. However, if such allegations are not disputed, there will be no decision on them.[54] And, therefore, there can be no *res judicata*.

The object of the dispute is, therefore, like a house of cards: the peak depends on the stability of the columns below it.[55] Similarly, the fulfilment of the obligation (main issue—formulated in the request) depends on the validity of the contract (preliminary issue—formulated in the cause of the request or in the defendant's allegation in defence), maintenance (main issue—request) depends on paternity (preliminary issue—cause of the request or defendant's defence), compensation (main issue) depends on the defendant's fault (preliminary issue), etc. Materially, if the validity of the contract collapses, the fulfilment of the obligation also falls. The same applies to paternity in relation to maintenance, fault in relation to civil compensation, etc.

[53] Mendes (1963), p. 294: "na orientação jurídica, o objecto do processo será a relação jurídica material, controvertida ou litigiosa."

[54] What can happen is logical chaining, "non-decisive conditioning premise of the decision", as stated in Sect. 4.2.3, supra.

[55] Another possible image is that of the tapestry: the thread that draws the main image is entangled in the threads of the scenario. Pulling one, pulls all.

Indeed, the *res judicata* that falls on the fulfilment of the obligation needs to fall, also, on the validity of the contract, as long as this, in the same way as that, has been disputed—that is, as long as there has been due process of law on this *point* (making it a *question*), with the opportunity to influence the court's conviction and to prove the factual allegations.

Therefore, the *res judicata* falls on the problematic material relationship in the process, whether through the main issue (relationship between request/device) or preliminary issue (relationship between cause of request/"foundation"—*rectius:* incidental decision). In summary: the *res judicata* reaches the decisions on the main and preliminary issues effectively litigated that resolve the substantive legal relationship, making it "immutable and indisputable", as the Brazilian legislator wants (art. 502 of the CPC). Or, as the Portuguese legislator conceptualises, the "mandatory force" extraprocedural refers to the "decision on the disputed material relationship" (art. 619, n. 1, CPC).

It is convenient to note that, by stating that the *res judicata* falls on the litigated substantive legal relationship, it includes the resolution of preliminary issues that imply legal valuation of facts,[56] and not when they concern the identification of the legal norm applicable to the fact, including its interpretation,[57] or when they deal with merely factual issues (the pure and simple occurrence of a phenomenological event).[58]

In summary, allowing the extension of the *res judicata* to the decided preliminary issues gives an adequate and sufficient scope to security.[59] Restricting it to the issues (main or preliminary) effectively litigated meets the impositions of freedom against excessive state intervention.[60]

4.4.1 The Ambivalence of the Incidental Declaratory Action

For a preliminary issue to be resolved with the force of *res judicata*, Chiovenda required a special procedure called "incidental declaratory action".

As indicated above,[61] the incidental declaratory action is a procedural incident initiated by the party who wishes to vest a decision on a preliminary issue with the

[56] Moreira (1967), p. 51.

[57] The binding to the identification of applicable norm and its interpretation represent the binding effect of mandatory precedents, having nothing to do with the legal regime of res judicata. Cf. Marinoni (2018), pp. 341–360. In the same sense, Mendes (1963), p. 461.

[58] Cf. what was said in footnote n. 48 of this Chapter, above, about the thorny issue of res judicata as a fiction of truth or presumption of truth.

[59] Cf. Sect. 3.2.2.1, above.

[60] Cf. Sect. 3.2.2.2, above.

[61] Cf. above, Sect. 2.4, about the incidental declaratory action. It is interesting to note that, in the portuguese CPC of 1939, the provision corresponding to article 91, n. 2 was article 96. However, the way that provision was written, as well as its location in the Code and the comments made by

force of res judicata. Article 91, n. 2, of the Portuguese CPC, expressly excludes the force of the *res judicata* from decisions on preliminary issues, "except if any of the parties request judgement with this scope".[62]

The apparent purpose of this institute is to increase legal security, eliminating any possible doubt about the incidence of the *res judicata* on a decided preliminary issue. The means by which the purpose of this institute is to enhance legal certainty by ensuring that (a) the issue is effectively litigated between the parties and (b) that it is effectively and adequately understood by the judge. In other words, the party's incidental request expands the object of the dispute beyond the main request, including the preliminary issue and forcing the judge to understand it, who, in the face of the prohibition of the *non liquet*, cannot avoid deciding it. Consequently, it is mandatory for the judge to decide on the preliminary issue, and it is also mandatory for him to ensure all the *due process* regarding the issue he will decide.

Now, if the *telos* of the incidental declaratory action is to ensure litigation and cognition, then what matters for the extension of the material *res judicata* is not the express incidental request, but the effective litigation and adequate cognition. There is no need for any other formality for the decision on the preliminary issue to be reached by the *res judicata*.

On the other hand, if there is no full cognition and complete litigation, the values of material security and procedural freedom, essential for the *design* of constitutionally adequate res judicata, are not protected. The "implicitly resolved issues" (such as the validity of the contract, assumed by the judge to condemn the defendant to comply with it) cannot become immutable and indisputable because, strictly speaking, if there is no litigation, there is no issue, but only a point; and, if it is implicit there is no cognition, but mere logical chaining, non-decisive conditioning premise. They would be issues simply *assumed* for the judgement of the main issue, without an effective and concrete judicial pronouncement for which it would be essential to ensure due process of law.

Professor Alberto dos Reis reveal that the intent in the previous legislation was very different. The purpose of the provision was to define the jurisdiction by the main issue, and authorise the competent judge to resolve all other issues and incidents raised in the process. That is, even if there were issues and incidents for which the judge would not be competent if they were raised as the main issue, he could resolve them, since the definition of jurisdiction was given by the request. However, the previous provision excluded the resolution of these issues from the scope of the material res judicata—that is, the issues were resolved only with an endoprocessual effect. The most interesting thing is that there were two, not just one exception to this restriction of res judicata: when there was an express request by one of the parties, as in the current article 91, n. 2, or "if the knowledge of the issue or incident implies the knowledge of the object of the action." That is, it seems that, in the system of the repealed legislation of 1939, the resolution of a preliminary issue (because it implies the "knowledge of the object of the action") constituted "res judicata outside the respective process". Reis (1940), pp. 69–70.

[62] A similar institute is identified in German legislation (§ 280 of the ZPO) and in Italian (art. 34 of the Codice di Procedura Civile), as well as other countries of Roman-Germanic tradition. The Brazilian procedural system established in 2015 abolished the incidental declaratory action, previously provided for in arts. 5, 325 and 470 of the CPC of 1973.

Analysing the German procedural ordinances prior to the ZPO,[63] Savigny observes an interesting contradiction.[64] Although it was expressly stated in law that "*simple motives should never have the authority of res judicata*", the same law allowed the judge to split the judgement to examine, in advance, the preliminary issues that he considered simpler or easier to judge than the main issue submitted for judgement. In doing so, as Savigny observes, the judge *decides* the preliminary issue, defining the right on that issue. In this case, the law would attribute the force of *res judicata* to the decision.

There is, indeed, a contradiction: if the judgement on a preliminary issue autonomously can be recognised as a decision capable of being vested with immutability and indisputability, then what would justify a different treatment when the preliminary issue is judged in the same procedural act that decides on the main issue? What would prevent the judgement on preliminary issues *in the sentence* from producing *res judicata*? Effectively, if there is *due process* and *decision*, there is nothing to justify excluding the binding nature of the legal effect produced.

Here is Chiovenda's contradiction: if the preliminary issue resolved by means of an incidental declaratory sentence makes *res judicata*, then why does the resolution of a preliminary issue by means of a common incidental decision not do so? The answer is given in Sect. 3.2.2.2 of this monograph: because social peace is not obtained only with security, but also with freedom. It is necessary to guarantee the *due process*: to contain the jurisdictional power within the limits of the request (principles of congruence and demand); to ensure the freedom of the parties to dispose of what they will litigate (dispositive principle); to preserve the possibility of the parties influencing the court's conviction about the object of the dispute, either with allegations (contradictory) or with the production of evidence (full defence).

In short, it is necessary to protect the freedom of the parties against excessive state intervention and to ensure the possibility that each one can calculate and decide the investment they will make in the litigation, in order to ensure everyone their day in court, "their bite at the apple". All of this is fully possible without the incidental declaratory action. It is enough to restrict the effects of *res judicata* not to the device of the sentence, but to the incidental decisions on preliminary issues, that is on points effectively disputed around which the parties have effectively litigated.

The above contradiction, attributed only for didactic purposes, to Chiovenda, derives from the mistaken indistinction between different types of "grounds". There are those that have been termed here "non-decisive conditioning premise" (for example, the plaintiff's ownership of the vehicle involved in the civil repair action, when not disputed). But there are also the decided preliminary issues. Issues, because they are disputed points; preliminary, because they condition the judgement of the main request; decided, because the judge cannot avoid resolving the controversy between the parties. From the moment the point is disputed, establishing

---

[63] Namely the Allgemeine Gerichtsordnung, I, 13, § 38, as well as the A.G.O. Einteilung, §§ 65 and 66 and I, 16, § 1 and A.G.O. I, 10, § 62, 81, b, c and § 63, c/c § 68.

[64] Savigny (1879), pp. 249 ss.

doubt about the legal effect resulting from a certain fact, it becomes a *question*, thus being the object of effective jurisdictional provision, expanding the object of the dispute beyond the main request.

But this contradiction can also be attributed to French liberalism which, in its eagerness to reduce state interventions in individual freedom, not only prefers to see the efficacy of *res judicata* diminished but also conceives it as a tool subordinate to the individual will of the party—an individualistic conception that, by ignoring the necessary solidarity and cooperation of individuals in a society has long been superseded by the model of the Constitutional State.[65]

Herein lies the ambivalence: the incidental declaratory action, created to provide more security, excludes the *res judicata* of preliminary issues resolved outside of the incident, even if there is full cognition and litigation. This paradoxically generates perplexity in practical forensic action: some preliminary issues are so exhaustively debated and meticulously decided by courts that it is hard to admit that they do not have binding force.

Because of this perplexity, Portuguese doctrine, recognising the need to endow such decided preliminary issues with the attributes of immutability and indisputability, developed the concept of "authority of the res judicata", whose obscurity accentuates the risk of false positives (issues not effectively litigated or not adequately known run the risk of becoming immutable and indisputable) and false negatives (issues effectively litigated and adequately known run the risk of being repeated or, worse, contradicted).

4.4.2 Brief Considerations About the So-called Extraprocedural Preclusive Effect

Although it is not the object of the present investigation, from what has been exposed so far, some considerations can be made about the so-called "extraprocedural preclusion" or "preclusive effect of the res judicata", in order to connect the theoretical proposal suggested in this study with that problem.[66]

For authors who argue for the existence of an extraprocedural preclusive effect, there is a *duty of concentration*, whether only of the defendant or also of the plaintiff, by which they must present all their allegations that possibly support the defence

[65] Marinoni (2018), pp. 172–174.

[66] For further insights on the subject, cf. Mitidiero (2006a). Sousa (2017).

or the claim, under penalty of preclusion of the opportunity to do so.[67] The preclusion would cover not only what was deduced but also what would be *deductible*.[68]

Thus, in the example of the action proposed by Maria against the painter João, mentioned in the introduction of this work, if the allegation that João's manifestation of will was not free and conscious was dismissed, he could not, under the regime of extraprocedural preclusion, seek to exempt himself from the obligation to paint the wall under the subsequent allegation that the price of the paint rose disproportionately (contract resolution due to excessive hardship), as this second allegation represents a fact extinguishing Maria's right already available to the defendant at the time of the defence presentation.

The point to be highlighted here is that the extension of the effects of the *res judicata* to the decision on the preliminary issue assists in clarifying the problem of the extraprocedural preclusive effect, highlighting the relationship between the two matters.

The central claim of this study is that the litigated and decided preliminary issue becomes binding in other processes and, on the other hand, those that are not litigated or adequately decided do not become so, and can be discussed again. Now, one might ask if this claim is not in contradiction with the doctrine of the preclusive effect of the *res judicata*, which prohibits the discussion of preliminary issues not decided or litigated.

Strictly speaking, in the preclusive effect of the *res judicata*, the deductible facts and grounds but not deduced only become prohibited when alleged *to attack the res judicata already produced* regarding the main claim formulated in the first action. That is, only to achieve the desired conviction in the claim does the plaintiff need to concentrate all the allegations that could support it. A judgement of dismissal that has become final in relation to this claim cannot be challenged by a different allegation from that initially presented by the plaintiff. And, only to be acquitted of the claim presented by the plaintiff does the defendant have the duty of concentration of all deductible allegations. A judgement of acceptance that has become final in relation to this claim cannot be challenged by a different allegation from that initially presented by the defendant.

In other words, a fact not alleged in defence, by the convicted defendant, cannot be alleged by him in a subsequent action *specifically to* exempt him from fulfilling the conviction. Or, reversing the poles, a fact not alleged by the plaintiff, in the initial petition, cannot be alleged by him in a future action filed with the purpose of

---

[67] In the Brazilian Code of Civil Procedure (CPC), there is an express provision to this effect in Article 508: "Once the judgment on the merits has become final, all allegations and defenses that a party could have raised either in support of or in opposition to the claim shall be deemed to have been asserted and rejected." In the Portuguese CPC, the provision that could be interpreted as indicating the existence of an extra-procedural preclusive effect is Article 729, g, a contrario sensu, which limits the matters that may be raised in opposition to enforcement proceedings exclusively to facts that extinguish or modify the obligation underlying the enforceable title, "provided that they occurred after the close of arguments."

[68] In Italian doctrine the expression "il deduto ed il deducibile" is consecrated, cf. Pinto (2024), p. 440.

attributing to him *that specific good* that was the object of his previous claim judged unfounded.

This *does not* mean that the issues not litigated nor decided are covered by the mantle of the *res judicata*—there can be no such *implicit res judicata*. It only means that the *res judicata* formed on the main issue decided cannot be attacked by any ground, even if it has not been litigated or decided. This system has to do with the protection of the *res judicata* produced regarding the main issue,[69] and not with a supposed—and vehemently rejected—"implicit res judicata".

Thus, the restriction imposed on João concerns more the obligation to paint the wall, on which there is a final judgement of conviction, than the allegation of resolution due to excessive hardship. What is precluded is the allegation in conflict with the obligation, and not just the allegation *per se*. João would be prevented from alleging the high price of the paint not because this ground would be "implicitly" covered by *res judicata*, but because it would be aimed at contradicting the obligation subject to *res judicata*. Suppose the contract imposed, in addition to the obligation to paint the wall, the obligation to paint the roof. Now, if the *res judicata* previously formed exclusively condemned to the specific painting of the wall, then there is no *res judicata* preventing the discussion about the increase in the price of the paint *for the purpose of exemption from the obligation to paint the roof*. However, if the defensive allegation of contract invalidity has been effectively litigated and rejected in the previous process, in which the obligation to paint the wall was discussed, then such an allegation cannot be decided again in the subsequent process, in which the obligation to paint the roof is discussed, as the decision rendered in the first process, even though it has resolved a preliminary issue, must produce *res judicata*.

That is, for the acceptance or rejection of *another* request, it is given to the parties to allege facts and grounds that they could have alleged, but did not allege, for the acceptance or rejection of the *previous* request.

Another example will help to clarify: alleging to be the holder of a credit of 1000 euros, X files a lawsuit against Y requesting its payment and obtaining the desired conviction. Would it be allowed for Y to allege, in a subsequent lawsuit, the invalidity of the contract that generated X's credit? Certainly yes, except to be exempted from the payment of 1000 euros to which he was condemned, not because the *basis* was, in itself, precluded, but because the obligation to pay 1000 euros is subject to *res judicata*. He could do so, however, to be exempted from the fulfilment of any other obligation, provided for in the same contract—as long as the validity of the contract had not been effectively litigated and decided, as a preliminary issue, in the previous action, as in this case, the preliminary issue would also be guaranteed by *res judicata*.[70]

---

[69] Alvim (2016), p. 622.

[70] This is precisely the example given by Mendes (1963), pp. 460–461, to highlight that the factual grounds are not covered by res judicata, except if the fact (validity of the contract) has been ascertained "in a regime of freedom of proof: then it will be a fact that the court has knowledge of by virtue of the exercise of its functions, and should be taken as certain by the court, under the terms

Rui Pinto mentions the German doctrine of the "contrary contradictory", according to which it is forbidden to postulate a legal effect that produces a practical result opposite to that stated in the decision that has become final.[71] It is precisely because of this prohibition that the facts and grounds not deduced, but deductible, are precluded: to prevent the legal effect produced in the previous *res judicata* from being put at risk. The prohibition of relitigation of the decision that has become final, the subject of the doctrine of *res judicata* is, therefore, complemented, so to speak, by the preclusive efficacy of *res judicata*.

Both Brazilian and Portuguese legislation, already mentioned, adopt this conception, whether by providing that it is "to the acceptance or rejection *of the request*" (art. 508 of the Brazilian CPC) that all allegations and defences that the party could oppose will be considered deduced and repelled, or by forbidding the defendant to allege, in execution objections, old extinguishing or modifying facts "*of the obligation*" (Article 729, "g", of the Portuguese CPC). In this sense, only the allegation of facts and grounds already existing is obstructed in terms of extinguishing or modifying *the obligation* established in the executive title, and not another obligation. The obligation that is the subject of the executed *res judicata* cannot be "attacked" in an autonomous action of objections nor in another common declaratory action, not even by facts or grounds not deduced, but deductible, not even indirectly, whether by the force of extraprocedural preclusive efficacy, or by the principle "contrary contradictory".

However, *another* obligation can be questioned, in an autonomous action, by facts or grounds not deduced in the previous action, for two reasons. First, because the controversy over this *other* obligation is not resolved with the force of *res judicata*. Second, because the basis on which this other obligation is discussed is not resolved with the force of *res judicata*. All this is based on the need to safeguard the value of procedural freedom, minimally. And to prohibit an individual from having his day in court represents a violation of the hard core of procedural freedom.[72] On the other hand, to defend oneself *from that* obligation embodied in the executive title, the defendant must have had his day in court. By not timely alleging that precluded basis, although he was given the opportunity to do so, he legitimises the restriction on his procedural freedom. In fact, from the waste of the opportunity to litigate, it is deduced that there is no restriction on the procedural freedom of the omitting party.

---

of the [old] article 514, n. 2." That is, if there is "freedom of proof" for the parties and "knowledge" on the part of the Court—or, which is to say the same: if the issue has been litigated and decided—then the issue will be covered by res judicata.

[71] Pinto (2024), pp. 434–437.

[72] Cf. Sect. 3.2.2.2, above.

4.4.3 *Brief Considerations on the Competence to Decide Preliminary Issues and the Effects of* Res Judicata

A final consideration regarding the present proposal is necessary.

Since the judge's competence is determined by the nature of the request (main issue - art. 91, n. 1, of the Portuguese CPC), it is possible that the preliminary issue relates to a matter for which he does not have competence.

For example, in the distribution of the competence of the Brazilian jurisdiction, actions filed against the National Institute of Social Security (INSS) are processed and judged before the Federal Court (art. 109, I, of the Federal Constitution of Brazil). On the other hand, actions that discuss labour relations are the competence of the Labour Court (art. 114, I, of the Brazilian Constitution of the Republic). Finally, actions involving the state civil status of people are the competence of the State Court (competence residual, Art. 125 of the Republic's Constitution).

Consider the case where an insured person files a lawsuit seeking recognition that they were working under unhealthy conditions, for the purpose of counting additional fictitious time towards their pension scheme. The jurisdiction to resolve the main issue lies with the federal judge. However, the examination of the preliminary issue, if posed as the main one, would fall under the jurisdiction of the labour court.

A similar case would be that of a person claiming a pension benefit due to the death of an insured person, alleging their dependency as a partner (stable union in Brazil, de facto union in Portugal). In this case, the main issue would attract the jurisdiction of the Federal Court, but the preliminary issue, if examined as the main one, would fall under the jurisdiction of the State Court.

Theoretically, extending the *res judicata* to preliminary issues could lead to a split in the procedural object and the shifting of its judgement to the competent courts. However, from a practical point of view, this would cause a disproportionate procedural turmoil, with the duplication of demands, and the process that carried the preliminary issue would merely serve as an instrument to the process that carried the main issue. With the turmoil, the workload, expenses, and time would increase, resulting in a loss of efficiency.

A pragmatic solution, adopted in Art. 503, § 1°, III, of the Brazilian CPC (and, in a certain way, also adopted in Art. 91, n. 2, of the Portuguese CPC), is to restrict the extension of the *res judicata* to preliminary issues only to cases where the judge who decides them has jurisdiction (due to the subject matter and the person) to know them as the main issue.

This means that if the judge who decides the preliminary issue does not have jurisdiction to resolve it as the main issue, then this incidental decision, even if it expressly resolves it and through robust litigation, does not produce material *res judicata*.

Thus, the two examples above represent cases where the resolution of a preliminary issue would not make it immutable and indisputable. The resolution on the insured person's exposure to harmful agents could be litigated again before the labour court, just as the stable union could be discussed again before the state court.

Both possibilities are theoretically acceptable. The more pragmatic one, however, seems to resolve the controversy more efficiently, being more useful from a practical point of view.

References

Alvim TA (2022) Questão de fato e questão de direito nos recursos para tribunais superiores. Revista de Processo 332(47):329–360

Alvim A A et al (2016) Comentários ao Código de Processo Civil - Lei n. 13.105/2015. Saraiva, São Paulo

Cabral AP (2012) Coisa julgada dinâmica: limites objetivos e temporais. Entre continuidade, mudança e transição de posições processuais estáveis. PhD Thesis, Law School at State University of Rio de Janeiro

Cabral AP (2021) Coisa julgada e preclusões dinâmicas: entre continuidade, mudança e transição de posições processuais estáveis. JusPodivm, Salvador

Carnelutti F (2000) Instituições do Processo Civil. Classic Book, São Paulo

Chiassoni P (2007) Tecnica dell'interpretazione giuridica. Il Mulino, Bologna

Clermont KM (2016) Res Judicata as requisite for justice. Rutgers Univ Law Rev 68:1.067–1.139

Guastini R (2011) Interpretare e argomentare. Giuffrè, Milano

Macêdo LB (2016) Coisa julgada sobre fato? Análise comparativa com o collateral estoppel de sua possibilidade de de lege lata ou de lege ferenda. Revista de Processo 260:355–412

Marinoni LG (2018) Coisa julgada sobre questão. Revista dos Tribunais, São Paulo

Marinoni L G (2016) Coisa julgada sobre questão, inclusive em benefício de terceiro. Revista de Processo 259:97–116

Marinoni LG et al (2019) Código de processo civil comentado, 5th edn. Thomson Reuters RT, São Paulo

Mendes JC (1963) Manual de processo civil. Coimbra Editora, Lisboa

Mitidiero D (2006a) Coisa julgada, limites objetivos e eficácia preclusiva. Revista Forense 388(102):51–78

Mitidiero D (2006b) Polêmica sobre a teoria dualista da ação (ação de direito material – "ação" processual): uma resposta a Guilherme Rizzo Amaral. In: Machado FC, Amaral GR (eds) Polêmica sobre a ação - a tutela jurisdicional na perspectiva das relações entre direito e processo. Livraria do Advogado, Porto Alegre

Moreira JCB (1967) Questões prejudiciais e coisa julgada. 1967. PhD Thesis (Livre-docência in Judiciary Law), Law School at Federal University of Rio de Janeiro

Neves AC (2010) Digesta - escritos acerca do Direito, do pensamento jurídico, da sua metodologia e outros. Coimbra, Coimbra

Pinto R (2024) A ação parcial. In press

Pisani AP (2021) Lezioni di diritto processuale civile. Jovene, Napoli

Reis A (1940) Código de processo civil anotado. Coimbra, Coimbra

Sarlet IW et al (2020) Curso de direito constitucional. Saraiva, São Paulo

Savigny FCV (1879) Sistema del derecho romano actual. Tomo V. F. Góngora Y Compañia, Madrid

Silva OAB (1979) Limites objetivos da coisa julgada no atual direito brasileiro. Revista de Processo, vol 15

Silva OAB (2006) Direito subjetivo, pretensão de direito material e ação. In: Machado FC, Amaral GR (eds) Polêmica sobre a ação - a tutela jurisdicional na perspectiva das relações entre direito e processo. Livraria do Advogado, Porto Alegre

Sousa MT (2017) Preclusão e caso julgado. Lisbon Law Rev LVIII:149–175

Tarello G (1980) L'interpretazione della legge. Giufrè, Milano
Taruffo M (1972) "Collateral estoppel" e giudicato sulle questioni – II. Rivista di diritto processuale, vol XXVII (II Serie). Cedam, Padova, pp 272–300
Taruffo M (2014) A motivação da sentença civil. Marcial Pons, São Paulo
Wieacker F (1980) História do direito moderno. Fundação Calouste Gulbenkian, Lisboa

Chapter 5
Conclusion: *Res Judicata* and the Binding Force of Preliminary Issues

There is no doubt that the binding force of a decision aims to prevent the judge from being placed in a position to repeat or contradict it (as expressly and excellently articulated in Article 580, paragraph 2, of the Portuguese CPC).

The difficulties begin when one asks *when* the judge is placed in this position. The answer given by the Portuguese legislator is logical: when the second case *repeats* the first (Article 580, paragraph 1, of the CPC).

This answer, however, raises another question: and when does a second case *repeat* the first? The attentive Portuguese legislator answers in Article 581 of the CPC: a second case repeats the first when the parties, the claim, and the cause of the claim are identical between the two, clearly and meticulously defining each of these three elements of the so-called triple identity.

Beyond the triple identity between *cases*, the Portuguese legislator anticipated the possibility that *issues and incidents raised* by the parties are resolved by the judge with the force of *res judicata* outside the respective process, provided that "one of the parties requests the judgement with this scope" (Article 91, paragraph 2).

The well-concatenated solution to the problem of the extent of the effects of *res judicata* given by the Portuguese legislator, however, lacks the problem of excessive restriction. Everyday forensic cases reveal the perplexity of the legal operator in dealing with situations not covered by this set. In many cases, the causes are not identical (in the technical sense of the Portuguese CPC) and there was no request for judgement of "issues and incidents" with the force of *res judicata*. But the judge often finds himself with the feeling that a decision made in a previous process somehow influences the case he has before him.

The perplexity felt by the judge, unable to frame the case before him as identical to a previous one according to the legal criterion of triple identity (Articles 580 and 581 of the Portuguese CPC) and of the incidental declaratory action (Article 91, paragraph 2, of the Portuguese CPC), has forced the rigorous Portuguese doctrine in search of solutions, such as the development of the ingenious doctrine of the *authority of res judicata*: even if the causes are not legally identical, and there has been no express request in this sense, the decision made in the previous case has binding force in the subsequent case.

However, with due respect, the lack of precise criteria for identifying the limits of the authority of *res judicata* has brought judges back to the previous state of perplexity, generating, as already mentioned above, false negatives (failing to recognise

G. M. Baini, *Objective Limits of Res Judicata*, SpringerBriefs in Law,
https://doi.org/10.1007/978-3-032-07485-0_5

the binding force of previous decisions that justifiably should impact on the subsequent case) and false positives (recognising the impact of previous decisions without a rigorously admissible justification in the Constitutional State, either by not observing the maximum possible material security, or by ignoring the minimum necessary procedural freedom).[1]

It is against such perplexity and indeterminacy that this study was intended, which, it is hoped, has served to assist in the analytical visualisation of this phenomenon, identifying, based on technical criteria from the conceptual repertoire of procedural law and the constitutional values that involve the doctrine of *res judicata*, that this perplexity derives, fundamentally, from the intuitive feeling that the case (or some of its elements) has already been technically judged.

The Anglo-American experience of *collateral estoppel*, demonstrated in the first part of the work, reveals the unnecessary attachment to traditional Romanistic conceptions and shows that it is possible to follow a different path, which better solves the practical problems that everyday forensic practice has faced.

The second part sought to demonstrate that the Anglo-American solution is not merely pragmatic, but follows a theoretical tradition very dear to the legal systems of the Roman-Germanic family, advocating for the maximum effectiveness of this fundamental right to *res judicata*, derived, ultimately from the Rule of Law itself. In the abstract weighing of the constitutional values in question, it was sought to demonstrate the need to confer on res judicata its optimal effect. Namely: to provide the maximum possible material security while ensuring, at the same time, the minimum necessary procedural freedom.

As I sought to demonstrate in this work, it is certain that not all the foundations to which the Portuguese Constitution (as well as the Brazilian and the American) would admit binding force. However, it is certain that some of them not only can, but *must* be vested with such authority.

Indeed, "grounds" or "foundations" of the judgement can be, but are not necessarily, mere logicism. The decision-making reasoning is directed at a conclusion. When it expressly resolves a preliminary issue, the judge is not merely reasoning; he is grounding, in relation to the main issue, but deciding, in relation to the preliminary issue. This becomes more evident when the preliminary issue is resolved in an

[1] Admitting the theoretical possibility of extending the effects of res judicata to preliminary issues, but as if lamenting the absence of legal basis at the time he wrote, Barbosa Moreira proposes, in 1967, the subjective solution, which has caused so much perplexity half a century later: "the natural reverence with which, when pronouncing a decision, the jurisdictional organ tends to bow before the conclusion established, regarding the relationship connected with the one it has to appreciate, in a previous pronouncement, especially when it enhances the confirmation, on appeal, by a higher organ. In such conditions, the absence of the characteristic bond of res judicata will not exclude the attention that the judge gives, in forming his conviction, to the logical authority of the preceding pronouncement – the stronger, of course, the more consistent the reasoning on which it is based." Moreira (1967), pp. 94–95. Now, to say that a decision confirmed at a higher level has greater prestige or to base the judge's binding to the previous decision on the degree of "logical authority" of the preceding pronouncement is excessively abstract and insecure. The intention of this study is to offer objective criteria for such binding.

interlocutory decision, separate from the judgement.[2] But it is no different when the decision of the preliminary issue occurs incidentally, in the same procedural act that judges the main issue.

In the introduction, the central question to which this study was dedicated was stated, namely, *Which grounds can (*rectius: *should) be covered by res judicata?*

Now, by way of conclusion, it is hoped to have confirmed the hypothesis then stated: only the grounds that are disputed by the parties, effectively litigated by them and expressly decided by the judge can (should) be subject to *res judicata*. That is, it is not about extending *res judicata* to the grounds of the sentence, but to decisions on preliminary issues.

The theoretical basis for such an extension replaces the question "how far does *res judicata* go?" with two others: "what do the parties litigate about?" and "what has the judge effectively decided?"

These two questions highlight that *res judicata* is not limited to the claim, formulated in the initial petition, but extends to all its assumptions about which the parties have disputed, with argumentative and evidentiary participation, about which the judge has expressly and fundamentally decided.

After all, jurisdictional protection is not limited to the portion of the initial petition titled "claim"—or even strictly to the initial petition. It is limited, rather, to the litigious object, wherever it may be found—even in the defence, notably in the facts extinguishing, modifying, or impeding the plaintiff's right, raised by the defendant.

---

[2] A significant example was given by the High Court of Justice of the United Kingdom, in the Queen's Bench Division, when judging part of the class action filed against the Volkswagen Group in the context of the so-called "dieselgate scandal" ([2019] EWHC 783(QB)). In this scandal, entities from various different countries identified, from 2017, the installation of a fraudulent device in a particular model of engines produced by the Group, which, detecting the testing environment, reduced power in order to keep the emission of pollutants within tolerable limits. In judicial and extrajudicial negotiations around the world, Volkswagen has already compensated victims and associations in several billion dollars for environmental, consumer and competition damages. In the case judged by the English High Court, the Queen's Bench Division identified a very significant preliminary issue and decided to split the trial: before judging the claim (compensation for the damages suffered), the controversy was addressed, raised in the defence, which aimed to undermine the basis of the claim, namely, whether the device installed in the engines represented, in the regulatory definition, a defeat device—that is, whether there was, or not, the practice of an illegal act. Once alleged by the plaintiffs that the defendant Group had committed an illegality, and having been disputed in defence this allegation, the point became a preliminary issue. The partial judgement, carried out by the High Court on April 6, 2020, was limited to resolving strictly this point, having concluded, in the end, that the defendants had, indeed, committed an illegality. Now, the binding force of this decision has a tremendous impact, because it authorises tens, perhaps hundreds of thousands of consumers, to use it to reduce the litigious object of their individual actions eventually filed, excluding the controversy over this issue and advancing to other points that may come to be disputed. It is not going, here, in footnote, at the conclusion of the work, to develop the theme of the extension of the subjective effects of res judicata. However, one cannot fail to provoke the question raised by Jeremy Bentham (see above, Sect. 2.3), compatible with the system of res judicata in the legal systems of Roman-Germanic tradition, as the extension of its effects beyond the parties, although it cannot harm third parties, can, in certain cases, benefit them. Cf. Marinoni (2016).

If the main claim is derived from a conditioning premise, about which there is a judicial controversy, then there is, in truth, an incidental claim about this premise. Such an incidental claim can be formulated by the plaintiff (who, in the face of a defence allegation disputing a premise of the main issue proposed, postulates that the preliminary issue be decided so that the object of the main issue can be attributed to him), as well as by the defendant (who, by questioning some conditioning premise of the main claim, postulates that the judgment of the latter ends prejudiced, denying the plaintiff the object of the main issue).

For *res judicata* to be able to extend to the decided preliminary issues, some requirements must be met:[3]

(i) prejudiciality: that there is a doubt about a premise conditioning the main claim;
(ii) controversy: that this premise is not assumed by both parties, but disputed by one of them (becoming a *preliminary issue*);
(iii) material legal concreteness: that it relates to legal effects incident on a material law relationship, and not merely factual or purely interpretative and abstract;
(iv) exercise of fundamental procedural rights: that the parties have expressly and effectively litigated about it, with the opportunity to participate in the formation of the Court's conviction and to present the evidence of their allegations;[4]
(v) competence: that the judge is competent to resolve it as a main issue;
(vi) material identity between issues: that the doubt about a certain legal effect raised in a subsequent cause is identical to that resolved in the previous cause, in terms of material law.

Once these requirements are met, the decided preliminary issues gain binding force both when they arise in subsequent actions as main issues and when they appear as preliminary issues.

It is concluded by stating that the extension to the decided preliminary issues finds the optimal point of the fundamental legal conformation of *res judicata.* Restricting it means deficient protection of material security; expanding it represents deficient protection of procedural freedom.

[3] All the requirements were explored at some point in this work. The idea of condensing them at this stage, in conclusion, is purely didactic.

[4] Although the subject has not been directly addressed, it must be recognised that, in this scope, it is also necessary to observe the legal procedure for defining the intended legal effect. In this case, the example often cited in this work applies, of the impossibility of recognising the defendant's ownership when he alleges the fulfilment of the requirements of adverse possession in defence of a replevin action. Although it is a fact extinguishing the plaintiff's right prejudicial to his claim, the adverse possession procedure includes the citation of adjoining owners and state instances, so the resolution of this preliminary issue in favour of the defendant could never produce res judicata.

References

Marinoni LG (2016) Coisa julgada sobre questão, inclusive em benefício de terceiro. Revista de Processo 259:97–116

Moreira JCB (1967) Questões prejudiciais e coisa julgada. 1967. PhD Thesis (Livre-docência in Judiciary Law), Law School at Federal University of Rio de Janeiro

MIX
Papier aus verantwortungsvollen Quellen
Paper from responsible sources
FSC® C105338

If you have any concerns about our products,
you can contact us on
ProductSafety@springernature.com

In case Publisher is established outside the EU,
the EU authorized representative is:
Springer Nature Customer Service Center GmbH
Europaplatz 3, 69115 Heidelberg, Germany

Printed by Libri Plureos GmbH
in Hamburg, Germany